PRAISE FOR *FIGHT FOR US*

"Marriage is one of the most beautiful and rewarding experiences couples can have, but it's also one of the hardest. It takes serious commitment to make it work, no matter what. Chad and Kathy are the perfect example of 'no matter what.' They've celebrated the best of life together, but they have also struggled through things most of us can't even begin to imagine. They've relied on each other—and, more importantly, their faith—to get them to the other side. Now they're sharing everything they've learned with the world. I know any couple will glean something from *Fight for Us*, wherever they are in their marriage. It's going to help so many relationships!"

—KORIE ROBERTSON, *NEW YORK TIMES* BESTSELLING
AUTHOR, ACTRESS, AND PRODUCER

"Never has there been a time in our country's history to strengthen the moral fiber of marriage and relationship. There are plenty of resources out there for married couples, but few are based on the harsh realities of the real world. And few are delivered by those who have earned the right to give those insights gained through extremely difficult battles fought and won. Chad and Kathy are dear friends. They are truly helping so many couples navigate and have victories in all areas through this new book. I highly recommend it. *Fight for Us* is a must-read!"

—VICTOR MARX, FOUNDER AND CEO OF
ALL THINGS POSSIBLE MINISTRIES

"Chad and Kathy's story is one of the most important one you will hear if you are married to a military serviceman or servicewoman. Take the testimony of this American couple and let it encourage you, strengthen you, and challenge you to fight for what matters most: each other."

—LIEUTENANT GENERAL "JERRY" BOYKIN,
US ARMY SPECIAL FORCES (RETIRED)

"Chad and Kathy's story is both heartbreaking and heartwarming. It is also miraculously transformational. *Fight for Us* is a must-read that will encourage you to fight for your family. It will strengthen your marriage and give you hope in the middle of a crisis."

—STEVE RIGGLE, PASTOR OF GRACE COMMUNITY CHURCH
AND PRESIDENT OF GRACE INTERNATIONAL

"I'm proud to call Chad a friend. His and Kathy's story in *Fight for Us* is certain to have a positive impact on the lives of veterans across our great nation. If you want to have an impact on a veteran's marriage, make sure you put this book in their hands. Well done, Chad!"

—ALLEN WEST, US CONGRESSMAN AND
LT. COL. OF THE US ARMY (RETIRED)

"Chad and Kathy Robichaux are dear friends and part of the WoodsEdge Church family. It has been my privilege to know them and pastor them as God transformed their lives and their marriage. It is one of the most remarkable things I have ever seen. God's hand of favor is on them and their Mighty Oaks Ministry in an unusual way. Read this book with an open heart and ask God to speak to you!"

—JEFF WELLS, PASTOR OF WOODSEDGE COMMUNITY CHURCH

"At a time when many consider the covenant of marriage to be outdated and unnecessary, *Fight for Us* points us back to God's perfect design for healthy relationships and nurturing families. Suffering from the lingering effects of a broken home and steeped in the often toxic masculinity of both the US Marine Corps and the Octagon, Chad Robichaux is living proof that no one, and no relationship, is beyond the redemptive power of God. He gives us a practical blueprint for success that is rooted in Scripture and tested in the crucible of hard experiences. We would all do well to heed this timeless message of hope and reconciliation."

—JIM SHANNON, CEO OF E3 PARTNERS MINISTRY AND I AM SECOND

"As a combat veteran, Navy SEAL, business leader, father, and husband, I have built my life on learning to lead myself out of hard situations and developing a relentless 'Overcome Mindset.' One of the most amazing things I have learned is that leadership is the same regardless of where it is applied—in life, in business, in parenting, and even in marriage! Chad and Adam have put together an amazing leadership blueprint, based on Christian foundations, that teaches you how to be a better leader in your family and marriage. Most importantly, *Fight for Us* teaches you how to FIGHT for your relationship in a healthy and positive way. If you are off course in your marriage, buy this book today."

—JASON REDMAN, US NAVY SEAL (RETIRED),
NEW YORK TIMES BESTSELLING AUTHOR OF *THE TRIDENT*
AND *OVERCOME*, NATIONAL SPEAKER, AND COACH

FIGHT
FOR US

Also by Chad M. Robichaux

An Unfair Advantage: Victory in the Midst of Battle
Path to Resiliency, coauthored with
    Jeremy M. Stalnecker
The Truth About PTSD, coauthored
    with Jeremy M. Stalnecker

Also by Adam Davis

Bulletproof Marriage: A 90-Day Devotional,
    coauthored with Lt. Col. Dave Grossman
*On Spiritual Combat: 30 Missions for
    Victorious Warfare*, coauthored
    with Lt. Col. Dave Grossman
*Behind the Lines: 365 Daily Challenges for Military
    Personnel*, coauthored with Chad Robichaux
*Behind the Badge: 365 Daily Devotions
    for Law Enforcement*
Prayers & Promises for First Responders,
    coauthored with Lt. Col. Dave Grossman

FIGHT FOR US

WIN BACK THE MARRIAGE
GOD INTENDS FOR YOU

CHAD M. ROBICHAUX
AND **ADAM DAVIS**

NELSON
BOOKS

An Imprint of Thomas Nelson

Fight for Us

© 2022 Chad Robichaux and Adam Davis

Published in Nashville, Tennessee, by Nelson Books, an imprint of Thomas Nelson. Nelson Books and Thomas Nelson are registered trademarks of HarperCollins Christian Publishing, Inc.

Published in association with The Howard Literary Agency, 102 Yellowood Drive, West Monroe, LA 71291, represented by John Howard.

Thomas Nelson titles may be purchased in bulk for educational, business, fundraising, or sales promotional use. For information, please e-mail SpecialMarkets@ThomasNelson.com.

Unless otherwise noted, Scripture quotations taken from The Holy Bible, New International Version®, NIV®. Copyright © 1973, 1978, 1984, 2011 by Biblica, Inc.® Used by permission of Zondervan. All rights reserved worldwide. www.Zondervan.com. The "NIV" and "New International Version" are trademarks registered in the United States Patent and Trademark Office by Biblica, Inc.®

Scripture quotations marked NKJV are taken from the New King James Version®. Copyright © 1982 by Thomas Nelson. Used by permission. All rights reserved.

Scripture quotations marked NLT are taken from the Holy Bible, New Living Translation. © 1996, 2004, 2015 by Tyndale House Foundation. Used by permission of Tyndale House Publishers, Inc., Carol Stream, Illinois 60188. All rights reserved.

Any internet addresses, phone numbers, or company or product information printed in this book are offered as a resource and are not intended in any way to be or to imply an endorsement by Thomas Nelson, nor does Thomas Nelson vouch for the existence, content, or services of these sites, phone numbers, companies, or products beyond the life of this book.

ISBN 978-1-4002-2820-1 (Audiobook)
ISBN 978-1-4002-2821-8 (TP)

Library of Congress Cataloging-in-Publication Data

Names: Robichaux, Chad, 1975- author. | Davis, Adam, 1981- author.
Title: Fight for us: win back the marriage God intends for you / Chad Robichaux and Adam Davis.
Description: Nashville: Thomas Nelson, [2021] | Includes bibliographical references. | Summary: "Introduces readers to a marriage challenge that not only saved them from divorce but also stopped veteran Chad from taking his own life and led them to begin a ministry that helps others fight for their marriages"—Provided by publisher.
Identifiers: LCCN 2021019730 (print) | LCCN 2021019731 (ebook) | ISBN 9781400228010 (hc) | ISBN 9781400228195 (epub)
Subjects: LCSH: Marriage—Religious aspects—Christianity.
Classification: LCC BV835 .R585 2021 (print) | LCC BV835 (ebook) | DDC 248.4—dc23
LC record available at https://lccn.loc.gov/2021019730
LC ebook record available at https://lccn.loc.gov/2021019731

Printed in the United States of America

22 23 24 25 26 LBC 5 4 3 2 1

CHAD:

To Kathy, for demonstrating what true love and grace is when I needed it the most. To all husbands and wives who have made a covenant to each other and to God himself, this is your call to battle; some things are worth fighting for, starting with the one you committed the rest of your life to when you said, "I do."

ADAM:

To Amber, I am incredibly and forever grateful for your unrelenting love and support for me. You have shown me what love means, and you make me a better man. To every husband and wife fighting the good fight for your marriage, do not grow weary. Keep fighting for each other.

A husband and wife may not agree on everything, but there is one thing they absolutely must agree on, always, and that is to never give up and fight for each other to the very end of their lives.

[Jesus] answered and said to them, "Have you not read that He who made them at the beginning 'made them male and female,' and said, 'For this reason a man shall leave his father and mother and be joined to his wife, and the two shall become one flesh'? So then, they are no longer two but one flesh. Therefore God has joined together, let not man separate."

—MATTHEW 19:4–6 NJKV

CONTENTS

CONTENTS

ROUND IV: ACCESS GOD'S POWER

ROUND V: PUT YOURSELF SECOND

FOREWORD

YIELDING TO CHRIST THROUGH SELFLESS ACTS, living by biblical principles, and serving God, family, and America—these are the phrases that describe our friends Chad and Kathy Robichaux.

I was introduced to Chad through a mutual friend and met him soon after in Washington, DC, when my wife, Jackie, and I invited him and Kathy to the Museum of the Bible. We learned about Chad's victories as a mixed martial arts champion and his remarkable service and eight deployments to Afghanistan as a Force Recon Marine.

Chad, after returning from his last deployment, found himself in a life-and-death battle with PTSD, the effects of which were destroying his marriage and family. But through the intervention of Kathy and Steve, a good friend and spiritual mentor, Chad embraced God's grace and restorative power. He leaned on his experiences to found a ministry, the Mighty Oaks Foundation.

Jackie and I hosted the premiere of *Never Fight Alone*, a documentary about Mighty Oaks, at the Museum of the

Bible. We were moved by the powerful impact Chad and his foundation have had on active duty and veteran military, police, and first responders who struggle with combat trauma, PTSD, and suicide.

Fight for Us describes the heartbreak and overwhelming obstacles Chad and Kathy faced in their marriage. It shares the life-changing biblical principles and "five rounds" of battle that led them to the strong relationship they have today, one that will leave a Godly legacy for generations to come. I pray this book will become a guide and a blessing to couples who feel their marriage is beyond saving and help them discover that God delivers hope and second chances to those who will fight for it—and for each other.

Steve Green
President of Hobby Lobby Stores, Inc.
Cofounder of Museum of the Bible

A NOTE FROM ADAM DAVIS

The true soldier fights not because he
hates what is in front of him, but because
he loves what is behind him.
—G. K. CHESTERTON

CHAD AND KATHY ROBICHAUX HAVE A STORY
that is truly captivating, one of the most inspiring I have
encountered in my career as a writer.

It doesn't matter what society does, how politicians
change, or what extremist groups try, marriage is, and will
always be, God's creation and his idea. He designed it so that
man and woman would be fulfilled and he would receive the
glory. God's kind intentions for marriage include promises
of beautiful things: love, joy, intimacy, and so much more.
Along the way, though, many marriages experience rough
spots, and only a few actually thrive. Why is this?

The Enemy wants us to believe that marriages can't
make it through the difficulties. He wants us to wallow in
despair, believing that marriage is a lost cause, too far gone

to save, and that there is no hope for the union of marriage. *But God . . .* That phrase is hope in two words. *But God* wants marriages to thrive. So do we. Which is why Chad and I have teamed up to write this book.

As a US Force Recon Marine and a mixed martial arts (MMA) champion fighter, Chad has experienced some exhilarating moments. But life isn't always built on the high places. Sometimes the best lessons are learned in the most difficult moments. And in this book, you will read about both the high and low points of Chad's life and his marriage to Kathy. You will read about his healing, redemption, adventures, and the hollow times when he finally realized what he had been missing. Chad carried some deep wounds from childhood and from eight tours of duty in Afghanistan—wounds that were sabotaging his marriage to Kathy.

Maybe you will be challenged by the question Kathy asked Chad while they were on the brink of divorce and, unbeknownst to Kathy, Chad was contemplating suicide: "Why don't you *fight for us*?"

We can gain it all, but if we lose the best parts of our lives in the process, will it have been worth the trade?

This book is arranged in five parts, each corresponding to five rounds of a championship MMA fight. Chad learned about these five rounds from a godly mentor who helped him develop a plan for his life:

- Round I: Believe God Loves You and Has a Purpose for You

- Round II: Be Accountable for Your Actions
- Round III: Accept That You Can't Change the Evils You've Encountered
- Round IV: Access God's Power
- Round V: Put Yourself Second

By the grace of God, Kathy didn't give up on Chad. And thanks to God's divine providence, they had godly people in their lives who loved them and walked with them through the valleys and challenges. Chad and Kathy's hearts were transformed by God, and God healed Chad. He healed their marriage and set them on a path of obeying his will. Now, they have deep hearts for God and a passion to help all marriages thrive, especially those of America's heroes.

We challenge you to read this book with an open heart and ask God to speak to you.

As I've partnered with Chad in writing this book, I have been challenged and compelled to become a better man and to work harder at my own marriage. My testimony isn't much different from Chad's, and that's the beauty of how two worlds collided. Although I never served in the US Armed Forces, I did serve in law enforcement for six years. When I reached the end of my rope, God used my wife to demonstrate unconditional love and show me a glimpse of his love. It was this love that saved me, redeemed me, and pulled me back from the tips of hell's furious flames.

Whatever you're going through in your marriage, don't give up; if you quit now, there are no rewards. However, if you keep fighting for each other, abundant rewards await you both. We urge you to enter the ring. Take a good look at your marriage. Better yet, take a good look at your own heart and open yourself to the challenges in the pages that follow. I count it the highest honor to be on this journey with you.

Adam Davis

How to Read This Book

WE URGE YOU TO READ THIS BOOK TOGETHER AS a couple.

Many couples find that being married doesn't guarantee quality time together. Chances are both of you are busy, so plan in advance to ensure you actually spend time together. Here are some ideas to help you make spending time together a priority:

- Find a married couple to mentor you. Seek out a godly couple to travel this journey with you. The wisdom and insight you can gain from those who have more experience can help you navigate these tricky waters.
- Read one chapter at a time and use the discussion questions at the end of each chapter to talk about the chapter's content. Consider making this a weekly date night as you discuss the material, perhaps even joining with another couple at a location away from home. Mix it up. Maybe go to a coffee shop one week and

a park or restaurant the next. Put it on your calendar and treat it as a very important meeting you don't want to miss for any reason.

- Take turns reading the book aloud to each other. One of you might read the odd-numbered chapters while the other shares responses to the discussion questions. Then you could switch roles for the even-numbered chapters. Even if you've already read the chapters on your own, try reading them aloud to each other; you will likely gain new insights or remember key teaching points when you hear the material a second time.
- Focus your attention on your spouse during your discussions. Be fully present.
- Be vulnerable and persevere. Everything you can imagine will try to get in the way of completing this book, but fight for your time together.

CHAPTER 1

NEVER QUIT ON US

IT WASN'T BY ACCIDENT THAT I FOUND MYSELF IN a place of complete hopelessness, sitting in my closet and holding a firearm, ready to end my life. Years of daily choices had led me to this place. But there was a breaking point, a moment when everything fell apart. It happened as I stood center cage after an important MMA fight.

It was August 2010, and Humberto DeLeon and I had just put on a show for over ten thousand screaming fans in the Houston Toyota Center. This was a big-time event with Strikeforce, one of the highest-profile MMA organizations in the world. I went into the fight with an undefeated professional record, having submitted all my previous opponents. DeLeon was fifteen years younger than me, and he was a rising star with phenomenal striking skills who had overwhelmed his previous opponents with combinations of punches or strikes. All the media interviewers leading up to the fight had questioned my ability to stand and strike with him.

Just as boxing matches take place in a ring, MMA fights take place in what's called a cage—typically an octagonal enclosure with six-foot-high mesh sides. Locked in the cage that Saturday night were two hungry warriors who both wanted nothing short of victory. While I was an accomplished grappler, a fighter who is able to subdue opponents with submission holds such as chokes and leg and arm locks, I wanted to prove my ability to take the center of the cage by trading punches and kicks with DeLeon. I landed some great Muay Thai "teep" kicks (much like a jab in boxing) that hit DeLeon square in the face. But just when I was feeling like I had the fight in the bag, I landed flat on my butt. For the first time in my career, someone had knocked me to the mat.

DeLeon then swarmed on me, and at that moment I thought, *How can this be happening to me?*

Now I was angry. It was time to turn it up a notch. Defeat was not an option and would only happen if I stayed down on the mat. I knew I had more left in me, so I got up and fought with every ounce of aggression I could muster.

Unless an MMA fight ends with a knockout or a submission, the winner is determined by judges. After beating the heck out of each other for three solid rounds, DeLeon and I were waiting for the Strikeforce announcer to reveal the results of the only split decision of my fighting career. I could feel my heart pounding in my fingertips, knowing how close the score would be. As I stood there, I vowed to myself that I would never again leave the outcome of a fight to the judges. I would never again leave that much margin in battle.

When the announcer declared me the winner and the referee raised my hand, the crowd cheered and applauded. It was one of the biggest moments of my professional fighting career, but I didn't feel elated. The only thing I felt was empty. I was empty because of selfishness, because of not being focused on the *most important* priorities in my life. I may have been standing in front of more than ten thousand fans, but the one person who mattered most to me was not there. I peered into the arena and her seat was empty.

Outside the Strikeforce cage, beyond all the lights, Kathy and I had separated, and we were facing a divorce. I was becoming aware of how badly I had messed up, and I was down on the mat in life. But unlike my experience in the MMA cage or as a Force Recon Marine on the battlefields of Afghanistan, I was unwilling to get back up and fight for my marriage. Looking back now, it's still painful to acknowledge the contrast between who I was in the cage and who I was at home. I was relentless in the cage, unwilling to quit after DeLeon's crushing blow and determined to win the fight. But when it came to fighting for my marriage and family, I was content to stay down. Instead of fighting for what was most important, I was filling the void in my life with all the wrong things—pursuing the wrong goals and fighting the wrong battles.

To this day, I wonder why I was so determined to fight for things that didn't matter and so quick to quit on my marriage. Maybe it was because it didn't matter to me who got hurt as long as I got what I wanted. Selfishness can destroy families and lives. When we live for ourselves alone, everyone else loses, including us, eventually. Had my priorities been properly aligned, and had my heart and mind been in the right place, it's possible that the career-defining fight in the Toyota Center might never have happened. But if I'd had my priorities, heart, and mind in the right place, I would have had Kathy by my side—and I would've celebrated a victory far greater than that match. I'd much rather be known as a man who fought for the best marriage rather than the man who fought to be the best MMA fighter.

Three and a half years before I stepped into that fight in Houston, I had arrived home completely broken after eight back-to-back tours of duty in Afghanistan. One day I was the golden boy of an elite military Joint Special Operations Command (JSOC) task force, participating in what I believed to be the United States' most important mission in the war on terror. And the next day I was benched. After my eighth deployment to Afghanistan, I was diagnosed with severe post-traumatic stress disorder (PTSD). My superiors pulled me out of the fight, out of my role as a warrior, and removed me from my team. I was devastated. In addition to my pride being destroyed, my dreams of continuing or finishing the mission to fight in the war against radical terrorists were crushed. I was in bad shape emotionally. In fact, I was afraid that if I allowed myself to fully tap into my emotions, to honestly express my feelings, I'd end up in a straitjacket and locked in a padded room.

As my life continued to deteriorate, I viewed the world and everyone in it as my adversary. Nobody "got it." I reasoned that none of this was my fault, so I needed someone to blame for the state I was in. If only my dad had been there for me as a boy and young man, my life would be different. If only my mom had chosen me over my stepdad, my life would be different. If only my older brother had not been murdered when I was fourteen, my life would be different. The list of "if onlys" was endless. If only my task force in Afghanistan had done things differently; if only my wife understood me; if only all these people had treated me with respect . . . then I wouldn't be in the mess I was in.

In truth, the downward spiral of my life and marriage was not the direct result of anything that had happened to me. It was the result of the ways I had chosen to respond to those events—specifically, the ways in which I had chosen to cope, seek comfort, and escape my feelings.

In retrospect, I believed the world revolved around me. By the time my life began to deteriorate in my midthirties, I was simply reaping the consequences of the choices I had made; choices that had put me at my own center stage for many years. At the time, I thought I was being strong, making choices that any "real man" would make. But strong was the last thing I felt when my world fell apart.

In the ministry I founded, called the Mighty Oaks Foundation, we ask a simple yet challenging question:

When did you become a man? The answers we receive are diverse, but most revolve around a macho "me" moment during the men's late teens or young adulthood. What most men fail to understand is that boys become men when they stop looking at the world as it relates to themselves and start looking at the world as it relates to others. Being self-absorbed does not lead to true success, and it isn't the defining characteristic of a true warrior. In fact, the opposite is true. Selfishness is one of the greatest predictors of failure, and true warriors are selfless. But these were lessons I had to learn the hard way.

Moving from "Me" to "We"

The summer of 2010 proved to be one of the most pivotal, if not the most pivotal, times of my life. Early that summer, a few years after my last tour in Afghanistan and about three months before the big fight in Houston, I was separated from Kathy and our three kids. I was alone in the closet of my apartment and crying uncontrollably. This was the moment it hit me full force that the common denominator in so many difficult moments of my life was *me*. There was no one else to blame. The realization was so painful I no longer wanted to live. The consequences of the choices I had made and the destruction I had left in my wake were overwhelming me with guilt. The thought came over me that maybe my family would be sad without me, but they would be better off, and that the best thing I could do for them would be to take my own life.

Around the first week of September 2010, and a short two weeks after the big Strikeforce fight, Kathy came to my apartment and unwittingly interrupted a suicide attempt as I sat alone in my closet with a GLOCK 22 (40-caliber) pistol to my head staring over my family pictures. When I heard her at the door, I panicked and hid the pistol under a blanket. Irritated, I answered the door, and we immediately started arguing. In the middle of that heated battle, she asked me a question that would not only change my life but also have a ripple effect on the lives of many others.

"Chad, how can you do all the things you've done in the military, Afghanistan, be willing to die for your buddies, train so hard for your MMA fights, and show so much discipline to cut weight for competitions, but when it comes to your family, you quit? Why don't you *fight for us*?"

She was right. I had never been called a quitter in my entire life, and it stung.

I accepted Kathy's challenge to fight for us. It had nothing to do with God at the time, but it brought out the same discipline and work ethic that had made me successful professionally. However, I knew I needed accountability in my life from people who would tell me not what I wanted to hear but what I needed to hear. I asked Kathy to call the church she was attending and see if they could find someone I could talk to and get advice, counsel, and accountability from. Kathy called the church, and the elder who answered was Steve Toth. He agreed to meet with me at a local coffee shop in town.

During our meeting I presented Steve with a plan I had written of how I was going to fix my life and situation. Steve briefly looked at the paper and then pushed it back to me saying I was going to fail. I remember being offended that he hadn't even read it, but I soon learned that his words would be life changing. He tapped on that paper and said, "If this plan doesn't have anything to do with God, I'm not going to waste your time, and I'm not going to let you waste mine."

By that point, I had tried everything—meditation, counseling, professional and financial success—but nothing had helped. We have a saying at Mighty Oaks Foundation today that came from that very moment: If what you're doing isn't working, then why not try something different? I knew it was time for something different, so I trusted Steve to lead me into a relationship with Christ. That began a one-year mentoring relationship that led to the restoration and healing of my marriage, hope, and a renewed sense of purpose that in large part has manifested into sharing what Kathy and I discovered with others.

Looking back, I'm horrified that I almost became a suicide statistic. Every day in the United States, twenty military service people take their own lives.[1] I would have left my children with that painful legacy, making them susceptible to another statistic: children who lose a parent to suicide are three times more likely to die by suicide themselves.[2] Knowing how much my children looked up to me kept me from succumbing to the darkness of my distorted rationalizations.

Through God's grace, I found the will to rise to the challenge of my wife's question. I committed to applying the same work ethic, discipline, and loyalty I relied on as a marine and a world-class athlete to my relationships with my wife and kids. I made the decision to move from "me" to "we." It was a complete shift of priorities. I would now fight for my character, integrity, faith, and family. I would use the same never-quit attitude I had displayed throughout my professional life in the place it mattered most: at home.

God revealed many things to me once I made this commitment and began to live it out. I learned that I was responsible for how I responded to my circumstances. I also learned that the hardships of my past no longer had to define my future. I couldn't blame my current difficulties on my parents, on my deployments to Afghanistan, or on some series of traumatic events. It was freeing to realize that the choices I make every day dictate the circumstances of my life, and that I have control over those choices!

Like so many others, I had succumbed to the pitfall of chasing the wrong source to fill the hole in my heart. Seventeenth-century theologian Blaise Pascal wrote:

> There was once in man a true happiness of which there now remain to him only the mark and empty trace, which he in vain tries to fill from all his surroundings. . . . But

these are all inadequate, because the infinite abyss can only be filled by an infinite and immutable object, that is to say, only by God Himself.[3]

I had tried to fill my "infinite abyss"—what many have called a God-shaped hole—with everything but God. The result was continued emptiness and frustration.

Several months after I'd been in that apartment being challenged by Kathy, I was sitting with a radio host conducting a live interview. As the host introduced me, he recited accolade after accolade: the titles and achievements from my life in the military, law enforcement, sports, and academics. After his long introduction, the host commented, "Wow, what a resume! How does listening to that make you feel?"

They were all good things, but instead of feeling pride, I felt overwhelming conviction. I felt like he was reading my conscience, or more specifically, that God was using his question to give my conscience a new revelation. I'm sure the host didn't expect my response, which was something like this: "Thanks so much for that warm introduction. When I hear all those things about me, I feel like a man who's lived a discontented life."

Without missing much of a beat, the host replied, "Well, you certainly have an impressive story, and your resume is incredible. Thank you for all you have done for our nation. We are happy to have you on our program today."

I am still working on how I should receive and accept compliments.

The accomplishments the host listed were great things, but, after my closet experience, I had begun to question my motives. Why was my life consumed with accomplishing one major achievement after another, never even taking time to celebrate before moving on to the next conquest? Even though I was focused almost entirely on myself, ironically, I felt incomplete. I had put my needs ahead of the needs of my marriage and family. I had rationalized my actions to meet those needs, even when they were immoral. The reason I found myself in the center of that MMA cage at the peak of my career *alone* was because I had made everything in my life about me. I had lost sight of what was most important, and I had lost sight of what I needed to fight for.

God gave me a second chance. I was given the opportunity, outside the cage and off the battlefield, to fight for what mattered most: the *us* of me and Kathy.

No matter the venue of your battles, it is critical to remember what you are fighting for and to fight for the most important causes. Ask yourself, before you flip another page, *What am I fighting for?* And if you're still down on the mat, *Why?* Now isn't the time to quit. This is your call to fight. And don't leave the outcome up to someone else.

My hope, through the words in this book, is not only that your marriage will become the best it can be but also that you will reach out and help other couples make their marriages the best they can be.

Fighting for the Right Purpose

You may never have been down on the mat in a cage fight, but I'm guessing you can resonate with being down on the mat in life. Maybe the knockout punches are coming from alcohol, prescription drugs, illegal narcotics, pornography, or something else. Perhaps you're reeling from the jabs of an unfaithful spouse or the choke holds of childhood abuse or sexual assault. Maybe you have PTSD from your service in the military, law enforcement, or as a first responder. It could be that you are your own worst enemy, and it's your anger, laziness, or selfishness that pins you to the mat every day. Whatever your situation, whatever your pain, and however it has impacted your marriage, know that you are not alone in the fight. Hope and redemption are available to you—if you're willing to get up off the mat and back in the fight for what matters most.

In the chapters that follow, I'll share stories and principles that Kathy and I hope will be both empowering and challenging for you as a couple. Our goal is to help you make your marriage all it can be, but that process requires a fight—not *against* each other, but *for* each other.

Just as there are five rounds in every MMA championship fight, I'm going to work through five rounds to help you fight for your own marriage.

Round I, "Believe God Loves You and Has a Purpose for You," will help you identify the source of your love and how you express love to each other. This may be a challenging discovery, or it may be a confirmation that you are already on the right path. If the two of you are in different seasons spiritually, that's okay. You can still grow together. As you progress, you will discover why and how your marriage is a part of a bigger plan. We hope that defining your purpose and discovering your role in that purpose will light a fresh fire to fight together.

In round II, "Be Accountable for Your Actions," you will be challenged to go all in. There's no such thing as fifty-fifty in a good marriage. No meeting halfway. You and your spouse each have to give 100 percent if you want to have a fighting chance at not only making it in marriage but also having a thriving marriage.

In round III, "Accept That You Can't Change the Evils You've Encountered," you'll learn to fight the right opponent. Spoiler alert: neither of you is the opponent. Sometimes marriage feels like a war. These battles and this adversity involve the rawest of emotions, which means you must do your best to manage those emotions. Know that evil exists in this world, and you can overcome it. If evil has had its way with you, we will share tools for healing and freedom so you can lean into your future together.

Round IV, "Access God's Power," will discuss how God provides couples with power to succeed in marriage. Marriage was God's idea, and he wants to be a part of yours.

The final, round V, "Put Yourself Second," will encourage you to be second rather than first, and will show you how to discover strength for every season of your marriage.

Just as marines follow rules of engagement for military conflict and professional MMA fighters follow rules for a fair fight, there are a few rules you can follow to create a safe place to learn and grow as a couple. Here are four rules of engagement as you make the choice to *fight for us*.

Fight for Us Rules of Engagement

1. *Find a mentor couple.* Find a couple you respect who is willing to be a friend to your marriage, not just a friend to only one of you. Arrange to meet with this couple weekly for six weeks to talk about how you're doing as a couple. You may find it helpful to use the marriage mentoring tools available on the Mighty Oaks Foundation website, https://www.mightyoaks programs.org/FightForUs. Make it a date night and commit to working on this important relationship in your life.

2. *Communicate often and well.* In any battle, communication is key. Throughout this journey, make time every week to talk about what you're reading together. As you do, be fair, open, and empathetic. Remove the words *me*, *my*, and *I* from the conversation, and

use the words *we*, *our*, and *us*. The greatest warriors exemplify sacrificial, selfless love. Use your words to fight for each other and for your future.

3. *Keep it clean.* You are one unit, one team, one body. Fight for your relationship, not against each other. It's okay to pause or take a break from a hot issue to get into a better mindset, but then start again—possibly with your mentor couple to help mediate a healthy conversation.

4. *Never give up.* Don't quit on yourself, don't quit on your spouse, and don't quit on your family. You'll bump up against obstacles that will try to stop you from completing the five rounds and keep you from working on your marriage, but commit to doing the work anyway. Be vulnerable together and persevere together. Believe in your marriage and make time for each other. Never give up.

Take the *Fight for Us* Rules of Engagement and apply them to your life. Allow them to serve as a guide for you on this journey. When you make the commitment to fight for each other and apply these rules to your battle, you are taking a giant step toward living your life to the fullest, together.

Each chapter concludes with three things you can do to fight for your marriage in everyday life: discussion, affirmation, and action.

1. *Discussion.* Talk about the chapter. What did you learn? What was helpful? Keep it positive. Use these discussion questions as a starting point. If you begin to argue, pause and move on to the affirmation section.

2. *Affirmation.* We are all subject to negative self-talk or comments from others. But such negative statements are not the truth. In this section, the suggested affirmations will help you to build each other up. Look into your spouse's eyes and say the affirmation statements aloud so that you affirm your love, respect, support, and desire to "fight for us."

3. *Action.* Good intentions without corresponding actions lead to frustration. Put into practice one of our suggested actions to demonstrate your commitment to your marriage and to build healthy habits that lead to desired results.

Now is the time to make your marriage the best it can be by fighting for what matters most: the *us* of you and your spouse.

DISCUSSION

- When you first met, what were you most attracted to about each other? Why did you fight for your (future) spouse instead of for someone else?
- What are some of your hopes for your marriage?

- Discuss the Rules of Engagement. How can you honor them as you go through this book?

AFFIRMATION

You are worth fighting for. *We* are worth fighting for. I am committed to our marriage. I recognize that we have challenges to overcome, but we will persevere together. You are important to me, and because I love you, I will not quit. I will fight for us. I will fight for our family. I will fight for our future together.

ACTION

Write out your responses to one or more of the following prompts on a piece of paper. Post the paper where you will see it often, such as a bathroom mirror or a refrigerator.

- The qualities I am most attracted to in my spouse are . . .
- A dream we share for our marriage is . . .
- The phrase I want to remember from the affirmation above is . . .

ROUND I

BELIEVE GOD LOVES YOU AND HAS A PURPOSE FOR YOU

CHAPTER 2

THE SOURCE OF LOVE

OUR UPBRINGING OFTEN SHAPES OUR UNDER-
standing of love and how we pursue it. Kathy and I both
come from broken homes, and we began our lives as adults
seeking to fill the deep voids that our childhoods left behind.
While Kathy strongly needed to feel safe and loved, I yearned
to discover and experience authentic manhood.

The emotional and relational needs of men and women
differ but are equally important. If you try to meet your
spouse's needs using the methods and sources that meet your
needs, both of you will end up frustrated and exhausted. We
are not commanded to meet every need our partners have.
Instead, we must acknowledge that true provision for every
desire and need comes from God as our ultimate source.
It is unfair to expect your spouse to meet your every need,
especially when some of those needs can only be completely
fulfilled by God.

As simple as this concept sounds, it took many years for me to discover it and to learn how to execute it. I lacked the fundamental wisdom required to lead my wife and children, and they suffered due to my lack of wisdom and understanding. It was impossible for me to give my wife love without first identifying what I was missing. When I found it, I discovered it was the very thing that equipped me to lead my wife and to find the true source of her needs: *our God*.

You see, my father, who had also been a marine and a Vietnam veteran, wasn't able to model authentic manhood for me. Looking back, I think he likely suffered the same anxieties and stresses I faced when I returned from Afghanistan, though I can't be certain because a PTSD diagnosis wasn't readily recognized and treated at the time. To cope with their trauma, many veterans of that era turned to alcohol, unhealthy relationships, and other self-destructive behaviors. I'm one among thousands in the post-Vietnam generation who grew up with absent or dysfunctional fathers, men who were incapable of providing a healthy model of manhood for their sons.

As a seventeen-year-old boy, I longed for that positive example. Since I didn't see it modeled at home, I thought, *Where better to learn how to be a man than the US Marine Corps? Ooh-rah!* How wrong could I have been? Very wrong, as it turns out. Listen, I *love* the Marine Corps. There are few things in my life that have made me prouder than earning the title of marine. However, while the Marine Corps does a phenomenal job of training young recruits for military service, it does not teach what it means to be an authentic man. Marine Corps training focuses on a concept of masculinity that has many positive attributes for success on the battlefield. But at times the culture of the Marine Corps suggests that a man should be measured by how many beers he can guzzle, how many women he can sleep with, how many fights he can get in, and how many f-bombs he can squeeze into one sentence.

Sadly, this flawed perspective of masculinity has ended many marine careers due to alcohol abuse, domestic violence, and other behavioral problems. I've witnessed good men lose rank over bar fights, families over adultery, or their health due to a sexually transmitted disease contracted from a drunken one-night rendezvous. Ironically, these behaviors that pass for masculinity are actually contrary to the core values of a marine: honor, courage, and commitment.[1]

In raising my daughter and two sons, I have relied on these values. My sons are now third generation marines. When my older son, Hunter, left for the Marine Corps recruit training, I wrote him this letter as a reminder:

Son, you are *not* going to the Marine Corps to learn how to be a man. You've already learned that from the model that God has laid out for you. Remember, they can and will teach you how to be a marine, but you likely know far more than they do about being an authentic man, a godly man of character. And now, son, show them how to be *that* man and let God's light shine through you, to be an example to your fellow recruits and even your drill instructors. Remember, Joseph was a slave, but God gave him favor as a slave. God used him to bring hope and inspiration to Pharaoh, the king of Egypt! Even when he was locked away from the world in a prison basement, Paul was able, with God's guidance, to light a fire under humanity to build the kingdom of heaven. It's amazing how God can use the least of us. Just as in those moments in history, God is still working through those who believe in him. And he can and will use a Marine Corps recruit to bring hope and inspiration to every soul you encounter. Never discount where God may have you at that very moment, for the very reason he put you here!

You are special and amazing!

I'm so proud of the man you've become and of your courage and boldness for him!

I am grateful that my sons say they feel loved and secure, that they don't have to struggle as I did to find out what it means to be a man. When I called my dad to tell him how Hunter was doing in boot camp, he said, "They will make a man out of him."

I was happy to reply, "Too late. . . . He already is."

Unlike my sons, I found out what it meant to be a man much later in life—but only after hitting rock bottom and almost losing it all. I have a good friend who says, "The thing about being at rock bottom is that it turns out to be a good foundation to rebuild your life on." So true!

My new mentor, Steve Toth, ultimately introduced me to what I had been searching for my entire life: a blueprint for authentic manhood. I didn't realize that it had always been available to me through Scripture. "Call to me," God says, "and I will answer you and tell you great and unsearchable things you do not know" (Jeremiah 33:3). Everything I needed to know about the source of pure love and the blueprint for authentic manhood was available to me through God's Word. I could ask God. I could call on him. I could seek the hidden things of his Word through prayer and study. By studying biblical principles about character, discipline, brotherhood, integrity, and marriage, I could be intentional about the legacy I will leave behind.

As I began taking an inventory of my life, I realized being selfish, chasing love in all the wrong places, and fighting for all the wrong things were not what made me a man. In fact, these pursuits were contrary to what the Bible teaches about being a godly man. These new truths I was learning gave me a standard—a biblical standard—by which to calibrate my life. I had come to a fork in the road and chose to follow the model of manhood that God intended for me. But it wasn't a one-time choice. Every day I still wake up to that same fork in the road and have to choose God's way or my way— though I now realize that there really is no life-giving *my* way. I've already experienced life without God, and I never want to go back.

I wasn't the only one who came from a broken home and a tumultuous childhood. Kathy was just two years old when her parents divorced. After her parents' divorce, Kathy and her brother lived with their father. After her stepmom and two new brothers came along, Kathy began to feel like an unwanted stepchild who was only in the way. Early on, rejection reared its ugly head in her life, and things only continued to get worse. At the age of ten, she was separated from her brother and sent to live with her mother, who had also remarried. These experiences left her feeling even more rejected and devalued. *Why was one sibling good enough to keep, but not me? Why wasn't I worth fighting for?*

Kathy's mother was a businesswoman, a manager at a bank. When she got home at night, she popped open a beer, reclined in a chair, and kicked her "puppies up," as she would say, while she relaxed and watched TV. Dinner was rarely ready before 8:30 p.m. Kathy ate alone at the dinner table each night, and her mother and stepfather ate on their TV trays in the living room. Kathy was out of sight and alone, rejected again. There was never any conversation or family bonding, which she craved.

Although she knew her mother loved her, Kathy didn't get the attention she longed for. Her mother was not compassionate or involved in her life, but she had no problem controlling Kathy. For example, her mother would threaten to take away Kathy's phone (a landline) if she angered her. Her mother knew Kathy thought that was torture! To gain some acceptance, Kathy did everything in her power to be a "good girl." Fortunately, she feared her mother enough not to become a rebellious teenager.

Today, Kathy longs to give our children what she never had as a child and teenager, so she strives to be present and attentive for them.

Kathy and I met when she was seventeen and desperate for some stability. There were a few boyfriends before me, but she was looking for affection and attention in ways those boys could not offer. Kathy says I was different. I was a young marine, and unlike the boys she had dated in the past, I was more mature and starting to establish my life. Her previous boyfriends had not cherished her, and they lacked discipline and work ethic. They didn't know how to treat a lady. Now, I was no Romeo, nor did I have all the answers on relationships. But I knew I wanted Kathy to feel important, as if she were the most important girl in the world. To this day, Kathy says she felt valuable and worthy for the first time in her life when we started dating. She called me her Prince Charming and felt that I had rescued her from all her fears. One year later, we were married.

It should have been the happiest day of her life, but Kathy experienced one of her deepest hurts on our wedding day. The twenty-year ongoing feud between her parents interfered with Kathy getting the wedding experience so many young brides dream of, and she didn't get her daddy-daughter dance. She felt robbed once again of the security and love she so desperately needed. That led Kathy to cry out even more for that kind of love from me, which put a heavy burden on our relationship in the years to come.

Now that she had someone to share her life with, Kathy

instantly put me on a pedestal. At eighteen years old, she felt she was finally on her way to a life happily ever after . . . *not*! As most young married couples do, we struggled. And when I couldn't live up to Kathy's unrealistic expectations, I felt angry and began lashing out.

Kathy began to feel rejected, and our life together was nothing like she had dreamed it would be. She dreamed of a marriage that filled the void in her heart with a man who would cherish her, a man who would selflessly love her. But that hole in her heart was back, and the rejection that came with it was stealing her joy. Once again, she felt ugly, unloved, and not worthy of anything good. She concluded something was wrong with her. *Why have I been rejected, abandoned, and hurt by people I love so much, so many times in my life? Did I marry the wrong guy? Did I get married too young? What am I missing?*

The Source of Love Is Always Present

When we married, neither of us realized that the source of love—what we were truly seeking—was already present in our lives. God was present. His power was alive and working in us even when we weren't aware of it.

I had experienced physical abuse from a Marine Corps Vietnam veteran father, abandonment by my parents, and great pain caused by the murder of my teenage brother. When I was thirteen years old, and my brother was fourteen, we set a goal to become Recon Marines and escape the physical abuse of our father. We wanted a change, a fresh start in life. When my brother died, the loss compelled me to fulfill our childhood dream, so at seventeen, I joined the US Marine Corps. After boot camp and the Marine Corps School of Infantry, I began trying out for recon and made it my first year in, though it would be ten years before I entered a real-life combat zone.

Kathy and I watched the terrorist attacks on the World Trade Center towers live on TV. At the time I was a sergeant in the Marine Corps and team leader at 3rd Force Reconnaissance Company. We knew our lives were about to change, and I was eager to deploy. About two years later, I tried out and was accepted into the JSOC (Joint Special Operations Command) task force.

It wasn't long after my pre-deployment training that I found myself in Afghanistan in a real-life combat zone. During the following eight back-to-back deployments, I served in a unique capacity that afforded me the experience of living with Afghan people, eating meals with their families, playing soccer with their children, and hearing horrific stories of what the Taliban had done to them. The oppression of the Afghan people and atrocities such as sexual abuse of children disgusted and enraged me. This changed how I viewed my mission. What started as a patriotic duty developed into having a heart to help these mistreated people. Where did that love and compassion come from since I had not experienced it as a child? It came from God. I believe

God put that love in my heart, and it manifested in the darkest place imaginable.

Whether it was on the battlefield in a foreign land or here at home in my own life, God showed himself in the worst places of my existence.

God's love is always present. All we have to do is look for his love and walk in it. This has been true going all the way back to the creation of the world. His love was present in the garden of Eden. In the garden, Adam and Eve had it all: a great relationship, provision, peace, and complete fulfillment. And yet, even in that place where God's presence abided, the place of perfect contentment and peace, the Enemy meddled in the relationship between Adam and Eve. The Enemy sought to destroy them from the very beginning.

The dynamics of their relationship were no doubt different from the challenges couples face today, but one thing remains the same: Satan's mission is to destroy the lives of men and women, including their marriages and families. If he can use an apple as temptation, imagine how many ways he can use the rejection and abuse of our pasts to undermine our relationships. And yet, even in our dark places, God is still present. His love persists. He is still in control. No matter how bad or dark your marriage may be, God's love is available.

So how do we access that love? How do we overcome the pain of abuse, trauma, or even rejection from our own parents? We can shake off any apathy and callousness and take one step toward him. "Draw near to God and He will draw near to you," wrote James. "Cleanse your hands, you sinners; and purify your hearts, you double-minded" (4:8 NKJV). If you want to live with God's love as your source of love, draw near to him. It's guaranteed that he will draw near to you. But this promise comes with some requirements: we must cleanse our hands, purify our hearts, and lay aside double-mindedness. In doing so, we are freed to pursue the true source of life-changing love with reckless abandon. Don't doubt God's love. Run to it.

Love Is the Only Option

If we are followers of Christ and have been redeemed by his love, we don't have a choice when it comes to love. Love is the only option. The apostle John wrote:

> Let us continue to love one another, for love comes from God. Anyone who loves is a child of God and knows God. But anyone who does not love does not know God, for God is love. . . .
>
> No one has ever seen God. But if we love each other, God lives in us, and his love is brought to full expression in us. (1 John 4:7–8, 12 NLT)

Did you catch that part at the end? John said that we experience God in this life by loving others. Wow! That's why love is not optional. Think about that for a minute.

When it comes to marriage, that means there is no such thing as "falling out of love," just as there is no such thing as "falling into love." Love is a *decision*—a conscious decision to reflect the one who abides in us, regardless of our circumstances.

John made it clear that God *is* love—which means, without his presence in our marriages, there is no hope for love to exist. Knowing God means we strive daily to serve our spouses in ways that reflect his love. Love isn't a one-time event; it's a behavior we demonstrate consistently over a lifetime. Without God as our source, we will constantly experience frustration, heartache, and exhaustion. It's in those moments that we too often become apathetic and lazy. We no longer pursue our spouses with the intensity we once did, and we become complacent, which creates resentment and hurt. And that can lead to fear.

We end up being afraid to love because we're afraid of more pain or of being wounded, mistreated, or abandoned. Cut off from the source of true love, it becomes all too easy to choose a lesser love, a synthetic love, to fill the void in our lives and numb that deep longing for the real deal. I have experienced this, you have experienced this, and so have millions of people who are hooked on everything from gambling to alcohol and drugs, pornography, and even work. Nothing compares to God's perfect love.

You access God's love as your source of love by habitually experiencing his love yourself. Let down your guard with God. Let your mind, body, and spirit receive his love.

"This is love," wrote the apostle John, "not that we loved God, but that he loved us and sent his Son as an atoning sacrifice for our sins" (1 John 4:10). Only when we see ourselves as *God* sees us, which is through the perfect sacrifice and redemption of his Son Jesus, can we love ourselves. Then we have access to the source of love that enables us to properly love our spouses.

Kathy and I are far from alone when it comes to growing up in broken homes with shattered childhoods and lives of pain. Many of us experience pain and disappointment and feeling unwanted and unloved. When we have not experienced love ourselves, it can be even more difficult to express the perfect love of God to a spouse. That's where Kathy and I were in our marriage. We'd both sought love in all the wrong places even prior to meeting each other. When I joined the US Marine Corps, I thought it was because I longed to learn how to be a real man. However, what I was really searching for was the pure love every man and woman should experience. And while I love the Marine Corps, all of us can experience this love without ever going through the doors at Marine Boot Camp and earning the coveted Eagle, Globe, and Anchor.

Right where you are, together as a couple, you can overcome the challenges of this life just as a marine would overcome any challenge or obstacle on the battlefield with training and preparation. In times of peace, when there are no conflicts or challenges in our marriages, it is easy to love. When the bills are paid and the sex is good, there's no fighting or resentment. But what happens when things go bad? What will you do if secret sin is revealed or an addiction surfaces? How will you respond when your spouse isn't easy to love, or you don't like your spouse for a season? That's when we need a direct line to God through prayer and his Word. That's when we need to remember how he has so perfectly loved us at our absolute worst.

When Steve presented me with the undeniable truth that God's Word held the blueprint not only for authentic manhood but also for saving my marriage and having eternal life, it wasn't a surprise. Somehow, somewhere deep inside, I knew it. Maybe it was a sermon, a song, a scripture, or a prayer I'd heard earlier in my life that had been placed in my heart by God himself. Regardless of where it came from, the truth was there. And I'm guessing I'm not the only one who's experienced this kind of knowing. You're reading this now and you *know* God's Word—you know that it has the answers you need. But maybe you've wrestled with it or fought against it. Maybe you've held God at arm's length, unwilling to connect to the source of love. Today the match is called. It's time to surrender to God. That's the way you can begin to truly and effectively fight for your marriage. Only when you selflessly love your spouse as Jesus loves you can both of you begin to grow together in him.

When we accept and receive the love of God in our marriages, it leads us to become a support for our spouses when they are hurting. We become the voice of hope and the vehicle by which the Word of God can be delivered, especially when they are vulnerable to the attacks of the Enemy. When we do not walk in the love of God, then husbands and wives, and their marriages, become sitting ducks for the onslaught of the Enemy.

The Enemy Knows Your Weakness

Don't think for a second that your marriage is off-limits to the Enemy. He will hit you right where you think he can't, smack-dab in the place you have that void. If it's sex, he'll hit you with an onslaught of temptation. If it's gossip, the water cooler at work will offer numerous opportunities to talk with folks who have no well-meaning intentions for you, your marriage, or your spiritual health. If the Enemy, who we know as Satan, could tempt Adam and Eve while they were still in the idyllic garden of Eden, we can assume he will do the same in our lives today. His strategies have not changed. He will always find a way to use our weaknesses and hurts and, through subtle suggestions, begin to create doubt and sow division in our marriages. His starting point will not be in the areas where you and your spouse are both fulfilled and content. No, it will be in the places where you already feel empty and are aching.

It might come in the form of a thought such as, *If your spouse really loved you, your spouse would . . .* Or, *Does your spouse really mean those words, "I love you"?* Or, *Your spouse didn't compliment you today, so your spouse doesn't really care about you.* He will plant those seeds of doubt in your mind, and if you're not careful, those seeds will take root in your heart and eventually blossom into sin.

The Enemy knows your hurts and your weaknesses. He knows your needs. He knows your deepest desires. If you aren't consistently and relentlessly connected to God, you are leaving the door open for attack and eventually domination by the Enemy. As Peter reminded us, "Your enemy the devil prowls around like a roaring lion looking for someone to devour" (1 Peter 5:8). Those are sobering words, but they should not be surprising.

Jesus didn't say we might possibly or occasionally hit a few rough patches here and there; he stated flat out, "In this world you *will* have trouble" (John 16:33, emphasis added). If you're married, you already know this as a fact. If you're a parent, you know this as a fact. If you have taken a breath today, you know this as a fact.

Fortunately, God's Word doesn't stop at giving us the facts about the attacks of the Enemy; it also gives us promises of protection, power, hope, love, and redemption. Just as Satan can plant seeds of hopelessness and doubt, the Word of God can plant seeds of hope and confidence.

"The Spirit who lives in you is greater than the spirit who lives in the world" (1 John 4:4 NLT).

If you are going to overcome the challenges you face as a couple and have a healthy, thriving marriage, you must surrender every area of your life to God. The places of need, the hurts, the unfilled gaps, and the unmet desires—they must all be surrendered to him and diligently guarded against the Enemy's attacks.

This might mean that you need to first *disconnect* from some other things in your life to truly connect with God. There may be habits you need to discontinue, relationships you need to terminate, or aspects of your daily routine you need to change. Other than God, what are you depending on to meet your needs emotionally, spiritually, and physically? Does your sense of fulfillment as a person come from a career, a hobby, or a secret sin? Are you depending on your spouse to meet all your needs? Do you believe that is your spouse's responsibility? What do you need to disconnect from so you can truly connect or reconnect with God? Only by spending time with him, as individuals and as a couple, will we experience this beautiful and life-changing love that equips us to move through the battles to come.

Imagine your marriage as a field that needs to be watered and tended to produce a good harvest. The harvest will grow from the seeds planted by your thoughts, words, and actions. If your irrigation system is connected to a source of tainted water, the crops will fail and there will be no harvest. But if you disconnect from the tainted water and connect your irrigation system to a pure spring, a lasting source of clean water, your crops will grow.

No field delivers a harvest overnight, so give your marriage the time and daily care it needs to grow. Anyone can read one verse of Scripture, close the book, and move on. Anyone can go to the gym one time. And anyone can make a vow one time in a marriage ceremony. But one-offs will not produce a bountiful harvest in your marriage. The faithful consistency of daily tending is key. You must be consistently connected to the deep well of God's perfect love for your marriage to thrive. That's how you protect yourself from the tainted water of the Enemy.

Today Is a New Day

You know the true and perfect source of love: a relationship and fellowship with God. But you may be connected to less helpful or even harmful sources. It's time to disconnect from those sources.

Your confidence will come when you know that God's perfect love is in you and that you have access to the power of the Holy Spirit to overcome all the battles you face. And you can learn more about that love and power every day. Never before have followers of Jesus had such ready access to so many books, studies, and teachings about God's Word and biblical principles. There's no excuse for *not* learning something, for *not* growing, for *not* filling your mind and heart with truth. The number one mission for each of you in your marriage is to dive deep and drive hard to connect to the source of love, so you can effectively love your spouse.

"We love because he first loved us" (1 John 4:19), and we choose to love our spouses because we know how well

God has loved us. When we make God's love our standard, we cut off the paths that give the Enemy easy access to our marriages.

Today is a new day. Choose to walk in God's perfect love, to learn more about perfect love in God's Word, and to demonstrate perfect love to your spouse every day.

DISCUSSION

- We've all made mistakes, experienced hurt, and been disappointed in life. How have such events shaped the way you experience love in your relationship?
- In what ways, if any, have you expected your spouse to give you the kind of fulfillment that only God can give?
- In what ways would you like your spouse to support you in remaining connected to God?

AFFIRMATION

You are worthy of love. *You* are worthy of God's love and my very best love. We are both products of his perfect love, and we are capable of loving each other well. Since you mean so much to me, I will strive daily to love you as Christ loves us, and I will fight to love you with excellence and purity. We are two imperfect people who will be a testament of God's perfect love.

ACTION

Love is sacrificial. It cost God everything when he gave his only Son for us. Love spoken is empty without love demonstrated. Every day for the next seven days, find at least one way to demonstrate your love for your spouse. It might be as simple as taking on one of your spouse's chores, giving your spouse your undivided attention (devices off and out of sight), or doing something fun and spontaneous together.

CHAPTER 3

FULLY COMMITTED

COMMITMENT IS A CRITICAL COMPONENT OF A successful marriage. Not a faux commitment in which words have more value than behavior, but a real commitment—the kind that puts others first, that asks for help when needed, and that seeks godly wisdom and insight to shape the future. We need a full commitment in which we willingly abandon any self-destructive habits, sins, and unholy desires for the welfare and betterment of our marriages.

Being fully committed, or being "all in" as some say, means we abandon anything—relationships, behaviors, attitudes—that does not benefit our marriage relationships. It also means we seek to have healthy relationships with individuals who will mentor us along the way. In the context of those mentoring relationships, we commit to being vulnerable and removing any masks that hide insecurities and unhealthy habits. Being fully committed means we bring our marriages to the feet of Jesus when we are down on the mat in life and the battle seems to be getting the best of us.

Before I surrendered my selfish ways and committed to pursuing my wife and our marriage, I used to dodge relationships with people who might have challenged me. I was willing to attend church on Sundays with my family because it was a way to ease my conscience and helped me feel like I was keeping my family in check. However, I avoided building friendships with men from church because I didn't believe I could relate to them. I used to think, *I have nothing in common with those men. They are weak.* This allowed me to control my circle of influence. I was a master at manipulating the influences in my life, and this eventually became a factor in my own defeat.

Once I separated from Kathy, I became reckless and turned to relationships with other women. I wasn't overly concerned about getting caught because I thought it would just expedite the inevitable outcome of divorce. Instead of confronting me about my sinful actions, the men I considered friends were willing to cover for me. They clearly had no concerns about my well-being or how my wife and children would be affected by my actions.

When we are doing the wrong things, we tend to want others to join in. We don't want to be alone in our sin! It's much easier to justify our actions when "everyone is doing it." After Kathy and I separated, even Christian friends wrongly encouraged me with comments like, "God has a plan for you and will bring another woman into your life," or "You got married too young and grew apart." Only one friend told me I needed to go home and do the right thing. Even though I knew he was right, I sidestepped his challenge. At that point, I was already committed to choosing destruction for myself and my family.

Even though those poor choices were mine and mine alone, I started to recognize that my friends were not really there for me. I actually wanted someone to tell me to stop, but I was alone and without accountability. It was a lonely place. The apostle Paul wrote, "Do not be misled: 'Bad company corrupts good character'" (1 Corinthians 15:33). Not every friend is beneficial, godly, or even good. Because I had intentionally isolated myself, I was surrounded not by friends but by enablers, men who actually encouraged my self-destructive behavior. After I had been in bad company with the wrong kind of men for some time, I eventually became one of them.

I didn't appreciate the fact that developing authentic relationships with godly men who would hold my feet to the fire was for my own health and protection. And so I neglected the brotherhood I had until I found myself alone in the lowest valley of my life.

Choose Real Relationships

Great fighters become great because they have great coaches, great mentors, and great cornermen to push them through the hard places in training and fighting. As we fight for what matters most, we need to surround ourselves with godly mentors, people who will walk through hell with us and be lifelines in our moments of weakness.

King Solomon, the wisest man who ever lived, wrote, "Walk with the wise and become wise; associate with fools and get in trouble" (Proverbs 13:20 NLT). That's the ancient version of, "Show me your friends, and I'll show you your future." Based on my relationships, or lack thereof, anyone could have predicted my future; at least, anyone but me. I was blind to my own destiny of destruction, caught up in selfishness and wallowing in sin. At my most self-destructive, I far exceeded the worst of the influences I had been exposed to. Even worse than abusing alcohol and drugs was the damage I caused by abusing my own influence over others and betraying those closest to me for selfish gain. The line that I crossed—the thing that led me to dive directly into sin—was choosing to spend time with the enablers instead of men of high character.

When I finally chose a new and healthy direction, I made radical changes to rescue my life and family. I knew then that I needed some serious accountability to sustain those major changes. Even though I had a thousand or more friends in my circle, I had no one I could trust to hold me accountable. What a pathetic place to be! That's when God brought Steve Toth into my life. He was the model I needed; he did the things I am sharing with you in this book. His life became a fantastic and reliable model for me to live out. Through being committed to God, studying his Word, and basing my marriage on my relationship with God, my path forward became clear. I needed the accountability Steve was offering; I also needed to follow the path of God's plan. What Steve said during our first meeting was true then, and it is true now: if any plan you have in your life is not based on your relationship with God, you will fail.

If you want the best marriage, you need accountability in your life. Mentorship is powerful because it demands authenticity, growth, and change. We all need others who will call out the fraud and lies in our lives when we try to hide them, but that can't happen outside of authentic relationship. In their book *The Complete Guide to Marriage Mentoring*, Drs. Les and Leslie Parrott wrote, "Mentoring without a real relationship is meaningless."[1] Real relationship is what fuels mentorship and accountability. If we keep our walls up to defend our selfish ways, we will never experience the best that life and marriage have to offer. But having a real relationship requires transparency and vulnerability. There's no point in having a mentor unless you're willing to remove the masks you're hiding behind.

Remove the Masks

When I came back from my last rotation overseas in April 2007, I had just been diagnosed with severe post-traumatic stress disorder (PTSD). I hated being labeled with a disorder, and I was extremely afraid of being exposed for what I felt I'd become: weak, vulnerable, and a failure. I was insecure and afraid for my future. So I hid behind the toughest mask I could find—that of a professional MMA fighter and Brazilian jiu-jitsu instructor. No one outside my home had a clue I was still struggling because no one could see what was really going on inside me. I was a fraud pretending to have my life together when I was falling apart—and my conscience and insecurities never let me forget it. To maintain the charade, I had to build higher relational walls and a bigger facade. I couldn't risk exposure, so I created a smoke screen of machismo and success. As a result, my jiu-jitsu school flourished, and so did my fighting career.

However, while my professional life grew, other areas of my life began to perish. My health, my relationships, my faith, and my overall well-being suffered, and there was no one in my life who could call me out. I had zero accountability. I had systematically blocked anyone who tried to get close enough to see the real me, especially anyone who might tell me the hard things I didn't want to hear but desperately needed to hear. As a result, I was surrounded only by those who puffed me up and supported my increasingly poor choices. They fanned the flames of my ego and enabled my selfish and self-destructive lifestyle. In life, what you feed flourishes; what you starve dies. I starved authenticity, godliness, and my marriage while I fed what I desired. And those desires were not pleasing to God—or to Kathy.

Soon enough, the walls I had built to keep people out came crashing down on me.

Wearing a mask is about hiding vulnerability with pride and ego—and there is no place for either on the road to healing and reconciliation in marriage. If you choose to wear a mask to avoid accountability, you will pay a cost—and the price could be everything that matters most to you. If you want to transition from brokenness to wholeness, you have to take responsibility for your actions and take ownership of your behavior. That's why I say I didn't become a man when I became a marine, went to Afghanistan, or won an MMA title, but I became a man when I stopped looking at the world as it related to me and started looking at the world as I related to it. I became a man when I took off my mask and embraced a selfless life.

I no longer wanted to pay the price of hiding my vulnerabilities and blaming everyone else for my circumstances. There was no one else to blame but me. The deception of covering my insecurities with masks had succeeded only in desensitizing me to the truth and to the consequences of sin. It led me to believe I was entitled to have my own way, regardless of the cost. The day I took ownership of my behavior, my choices, and my marriage was the day I took a step toward freedom and a real life.

You may think your masks are helping you to win in life, especially if they help you to achieve success in some way, as mine did for a time. But when you walk around with a mask on, you are already defeated. You are already dead. You are already a loser. The winning choice is to willingly raise your hands in surrender and say to the Lord, "Not my will, but yours be done" (Luke 22:42). That's when you truly begin to live. One of the bravest things you will ever do is set aside the masks and own up to your choices and behaviors.

Make Course Corrections

Throughout this book, I have shared and will share how God redeemed me. In 2010, about three years after my last deployment, an affair with another woman was brought to light, and Kathy and I decided to separate and file for divorce. That's when I signed on for the big Strikeforce fight in Houston, Texas. You've learned a lot about my life through my career in the marines and as an MMA fighter, but I believe the most important lesson you can take away from it is how I made course corrections away from the darkest places, the places with incredible pain.

It would be easy to blame all my behavior on the PTSD diagnosis I received in 2007 or on panic disorder, anxiety, and shame. It would be easy to point fingers at other reasons I was unfaithful to Kathy and God, but at the end of the day, I was forced to recognize my own sin. When I met Steve in 2010, at my absolute rock bottom, my mind and heart were ready to change. I just didn't know how to change. I knew it would take incredible sacrifice on my part, but where was I supposed to start?

Steve led me through a series of steps. The first was giving my life to Christ, which meant every single decision going forward had to be based on my relationship with him. Then we began a one-year mentoring relationship, where Steve discipled me in my walk with Christ and in my reconciliation with Kathy.

When we are forced to come face-to-face with the consequences of our decisions, we can cower down or be courageous and face them head on. It requires courage to admit when you need a course correction. It requires courage to admit when you need help. It's okay to say, "I know I need help, but I am not sure what to do next." Looking back, it was only the grace and mercy of God that preserved me through these corrections in my life. Your past, your sin, your incredibly terrible decisions don't have to be the defining moments in your life.

Repentance, which means to change direction, is the next step. Change your heart and mind, do a one-eighty, and go the other way. Surrender to Christ, find a mentor, admit you need course correction, and repent. Then walk in the new life you have been given.

Through my quest to become the man, husband, father, and leader that God created me to be, I've come to a deeper revelation of what it means to take full responsibility for my life. Now, when I look at the flaws of those God has entrusted me to lead, I have a much more tolerant approach. I think about Paul's letter to the Romans, "Therefore, I urge you, brothers and sisters, in view of God's mercy, to offer your bodies as a living sacrifice, holy and pleasing to

God—this is your true and proper worship" (Romans 12:1). This is the way we should pursue living—knowing our bodies are *his* and we are merely stewards. Of course, as a leader I hold others accountable, but I also assess each situation to understand how I, too, could have done things better. This heightened understanding has been a game changer for me. I thank God for opening my eyes to my own faults and responsibilities and for giving me a second chance to lead my family the way he intended.

Now, I have more patience, grace, and understanding for the shortcomings of others. While working with others who struggle in the same way, I can see that God-shaped hole clearly. I observe as couples try everything but God to fill that hole. These efforts to fill that void often make things worse . . . much worse. What I have learned is that you can't pour enough liquor, dump enough pills, or throw enough sex, fame, fortune, adventure, or success at it! A God-shaped hole is reserved for one thing, and that is Jesus Christ alone. Without him, there will always be emptiness, a longing desire, a thirst never quenched, an itch never scratched, and a hole never filled.

I was no different. After getting medications prescribed to numb the anxiety, I was well on my way to finding something to fill that void.

Throughout my entire life, I had trained in martial arts and had a deep-rooted passion for Brazilian jiu-jitsu (BJJ), so I had a head start on getting plugged into a new chapter in my life after the military. Finally, I could be the "cool guy" again! On a mountain on the other side of the world, I had lost some of my ego, and this was an opportunity for me to rebuild it once and for all. I wanted so badly to be respected. Kathy and I opened an MMA school and ran it as a family business; we were living the American dream. What we didn't know was that I was not in a position to handle the success that would come with it. I was still broken, not healed by God, and certainly walking outside of his will for my life.

The school's success was incredible. We opened with 180 students, and in three years, we had one of the biggest BJJ/MMA schools in America at the time, with an enrollment of approximately 900 students in two locations. I had received my BJJ black belt in Brazil, I had won an MMA world championship under the Legacy Fighting Alliance banner (formerly Legacy Fighting Championship), and I was undefeated as a pro and top ranked in my division. The world was in the palm of my hand, and everything was perfect.

In reality, that was far from the truth. Although on the surface everything looked perfect, my life was far from it. I was living a lie. Instead of liquor or excessive drug use, I had isolated myself in a fake world of success. I was a mess, and I was angry.

My house was not a happy place, and my wife and kids were afraid of me. Kathy and I lived separate lives in our own home. I still felt as if I had failed at my mission and didn't even want to speak of my past military service. I was ashamed. I was terrified of my mental health condition, of having additional panic attacks or sleepless nights, so I ran from those fears by keeping myself as busy as possible. I had put myself in a position of zero accountability—in a world where everyone lifts you up and tells you what you want to hear, but no one tells you what you need to hear.

I had chased and caught a false god of success, and it was unfulfilling. The temporary high of a moment in the spotlight not only allowed the void to remain but also caused it to grow. Kathy and I were worlds apart. It didn't take long for temptation to overtake me, and I did something I never thought I would do. I turned outside of my marriage for attention and relationships with other women, and eventually separated from Kathy and the kids.

Good medicine can be abused, and that is what I did. I used it out of context. My medicine was martial arts. I loved it. I still love it, and I'm still involved with it. But in the early years, like many things in my life, I used worldly endeavors in an attempt to fill a void in my life that only God could fill. Once again, I was left empty and hopeless, even at the top of my pro MMA career. What a joy it is now to live a life fulfilled by God, who meets all my needs, heals all my hurts, and covers all my fears and anxieties. He is the only one who can heal the wounds we hide under the masks, straighten our crooked paths, and lead us into our destiny of victory.

Keep Doing the Hard Work

One of the most important steps you can take for your marriage is to eliminate relationships that are not beneficial to your marriage. This means that if your friends do not provide a positive contribution to your marriage, it may be time to distance yourself from them. If they have toxic habits that you have specifically dealt with and you are not in a position to overcome those temptations, it would be wise to create distance from those relationships. And use extreme caution when having relationships outside of professional interactions with individuals of the opposite sex.

Ultimately, if any of your relationships are beneficial to you as an individual but wouldn't push you to fight for your family, you need to cut ties. This means ditching the friends who want you to "hang out" or "have a few," which leads to long nights and endless fights with your spouse. That's a hard truth, but it is *the* truth.

Marriage is a lifelong process of learning to see the needs of another person as more important than your own. This is difficult because it's not natural. Thinking this way requires the kind of change that can be made only through the power of God at work in your life. Pastor and author Andy Stanley once said, "Christian marriage is a submission competition. A race to the back of the line!"[2] And being intentional with your words, actions, habits, and relationships is part of the race, the hard work necessary to have a thriving marriage.

A little bit of empathy goes a long way when it comes to your marriage. Think about it like this: How would it make you feel if your spouse was spending time with someone who had a bad habit or someone of the opposite sex? How would it make you feel if your spouse was spending more time with "friends" and hobbies than with you? It's common courtesy to be intentional with your relationships. So honor your spouse by doing the hard work necessary to have a healthy marriage and respect your commitment to each other.

It seems like common sense to show courtesy to the one you promised to spend the rest of your life with. But for some of us, once the vows are exchanged, our brain cells disappear and are backfilled with selfishness and pride. We no longer pursue our spouses or put in the work required to have a thriving marriage. Then it isn't long until we become bitter, jaded, and resentful, especially when we see other couples who are thriving and happy. We forget that marriage requires work—a commitment to keep pursuing our spouses. Commitment isn't what we need when things are easy; it is what we need when things get hard, when we want to quit. Commitment reminds us *why* we chose to do life together. Commitment is having a battle plan for when life punches you in the mouth.

Together, you and your spouse can make it. If honoring your commitment is a priority, if you're willing to fight for it, you truly can have the happiest, healthiest, and most fulfilling marriage.

DISCUSSION

- How do you feel about the prospect of allowing a mentor or friend to challenge you to live a more

godly life? How do you feel about mentoring someone and helping them to live a more godly life?

- Briefly identify and list three to five friends. In what
ways, if any, is each person a friend to your marriage? In what ways, if any, is each person a bad
influence?

- Being fully committed means letting go of
anything—relationships, behaviors, attitudes—
that does not benefit your relationship. What might
you have to let go of to be fully committed to your
marriage?

- How would you describe your commitment to your
spouse to refocus your priorities?

AFFIRMATION

God never called us to live in isolation or to battle
alone. He has given us the wisdom and willpower to
address the hard issues in life. But we need to do it as a
team, husband and wife, surrendered to God.

ACTION

- When you notice your spouse drifting, draw near
to them with compassion and love. This is part
of your commitment as a couple, to be present
when one of you is suffering or when life becomes
challenging.

- Identify ways you can increase your commitment to your marriage using the following as your baseline:
  › Commit the past to God through mutual forgiveness. Talk with your spouse and mentors about how you can most effectively address this issue.
  › Commit to the future of your marriage through godly marriage mentorship.
  › Commit to being authentic with each other. Consider this question as a starting place: *How can I best be authentic with you, so my commitment is known and I am not passive in addressing the challenges we face?*
- If you named any relationships, behaviors, or attitudes that are not good for your marriage in the discussion section above, identify at least one step you will take within the next week to let go of whatever that is. You demonstrate commitment when you surrender anything that is not leading you closer to Christ and to having a better marriage.

ROUND II

BE ACCOUNTABLE
FOR YOUR ACTIONS

CHAPTER 4

Prepare for Battle

I HAVE SPENT MUCH OF MY LIFE PREPARING FOR one battle or another, whether it was a martial arts competition, an MMA fight, or a military deployment. When preparing for war, fighting the *right* enemy is critical. But too often that enemy is right between our ears, or we give the Enemy access to our minds and he runs with it.

While deployed in Afghanistan, my team didn't operate in a conventional role. We were usually embedded with local nationals and wore civilian or even local clothing. On several occasions we had to purchase large amounts of local guns and ammunition. We bought everything from AK-47 assault rifles and PKM machine guns to the occasional RPGs (rocket-propelled grenade launchers) to cache in safe houses and clandestine FOBs (forward operating bases) for our task force. Assignments like gun buys were routine enough that it was easy to be complacent, to forget how dangerous things really were. But in a setting like Afghanistan, complacency can be fatal.

I had a very close call once when preparing to buy weapons from a new contact named Ahmed, the nephew of a tribal village elder we knew and trusted. I had initially planned to go on my own, taking along only our Afghan translator, Aziz, who had become like a brother to our team. But both Aziz and I had a sense that maybe that wasn't the best idea, so I asked Dano and Bink, two other members of our team, to come along.

As we pulled into Ahmed's dilapidated mud compound off a remote road west of Kabul, I immediately had the sense that something was off. Ahmed was waiting in his SUV at the center of the compound, but he seemed overly nervous. While Dano, who speaks fluent Dari, and I went to talk with him, Bink and Aziz took up security, watching the access area in front to ensure we had no surprise visitors, a decision that likely saved our lives.

As Dano and Ahmed began to talk money, Bink and Aziz suddenly began yelling. Then they pointed their rifles toward an approaching Toyota Corolla occupied by four tribally dressed Afghans armed with AK-47s. Because Bink and Aziz had the drop on the vehicle, it couldn't advance. But Ahmed, who couldn't see the vehicle, began yelling, "Don't hurt them! They are my friends!"

"Who'd you bring here?" Dano asked Ahmed.

When Ahmed didn't answer, we knew the whole thing had been a setup. Dano grabbed him and stuck his pistol to the side of Ahmed's neck while I ran over to help Bink and Aziz. After covering one another to maneuver and seize control of the Corolla, we disarmed the occupants, removed them from the vehicle, and zip-tied their hands behind their backs. Bink moved the Corolla to clear the exit to the compound and tossed the car keys far into the brush. We forced the four occupants face down into a roadside ditch where they stayed until we were long gone.

Aziz then took control of Ahmed, who was now also zip-tied, and shoved him in the back seat of our SUV as everyone loaded in. Dano drove while Aziz interrogated Ahmed about why he set us up and tried to rob us. Ultimately, Ahmed's reasoning was that he assumed he was meeting me alone and thought he could take advantage of me being outnumbered and surprised. We decided the best penalty would be to turn Ahmed over to his uncle and tell him what had happened. We never heard from or of him again.

The Real Enemy of Your Marriage

After every operation, our team did a debriefing to develop an after-action report (AAR). We looked at what went wrong, what went right, what could be improved, and what needed to change. I learned some life-saving principles from those debriefs over the years, including remembering that if we saw one weapon, we should assume there were two, and to never be complacent in dangerous territory. I almost made the fatal mistake of going on that gun buy with only Aziz. If we had not taken along Dano and Bink that day, we likely would have been killed or taken hostage.

Whether in combat or in life, complacency can be fatal. And when it comes to marriage, we have to remember that we live in a hostile environment with a spiritual Enemy who wants nothing more than to find us alone and complacent.

The ultimate mission of every believer is to reach the world for Jesus by loving God and loving others as we love ourselves. Our starting point for loving others, what we might call mission one, is our spouses and families. Because we live in a world that is hostile to the things of God, we have to remember that the Enemy wants us to fail. The challenge is that we cannot see this Enemy, which makes the battle exponentially more difficult. It also increases the odds that we'll get confused about who we're fighting.

If you've been married for any length of time, chances are you've had times when it seems as though your spouse is the enemy standing in the way of what you want, of getting your needs met, or of having a thriving relationship. You will without a doubt experience challenges in your job or in other relationships, but you will face immeasurable challenges in your marriage, especially if you want to have a relationship that is more than just getting by. Listen, in your marriage, it may seem as if the quirks or habits you once admired and loved about each other are the enemies, or maybe your past mistakes or those of your spouse are the enemies. Whenever that happens, pay attention, because it's a warning sign that an Enemy is definitely at work in your marriage. But know that your spouse is not that enemy. The real Enemy of your marriage is unseen.

It is critical for us to identify the real Enemy in our lives, the one who wants to completely annihilate our marriages, our families, and our futures. After that we can better identify and recognize his strategies. Marriage empowers us to join forces so that we can fight together and fight for—rather than against—each other. Remember, God can use willing vessels, but so can the Enemy.

Two of the Enemy's most effective sabotage strategies in marriage are using selfishness and pride. To get an idea of how effective these strategies are, consider how they might have led to a very different outcome in that gun buy in Afghanistan. Can you imagine what would have happened if Bink and Aziz, instead of raising the alarm and pinning down the approaching car, had seen the enemy coming and taken off to save their own skins? What if I had decided to go to the buy on my own because I thought taking along Bink and Dano made me look weak? Fortunately, neither of those things happened. There wasn't a selfish or prideful person on our team. In fact, it was selflessness and humility that preserved us. It was the wisdom of selflessness and humility that kept us from being complacent in hostile territory. And the same principles apply in marriage. Selflessness and humility will help you and your spouse to be united and focused on the real threat to your marriage.

Maybe you feel like your marriage is akin to a team of

operators on a mission gone bad overseas, or you feel like the fighter on the mat in the cage. Maybe your marriage went wrong somewhere along the way, and you're wondering just how it all happened. No matter what you're dealing with today, know who the real Enemy is in your marriage. Satan will deploy the weapons of selfishness, pride, and complacency at every turn. He will use subtle hints and suggestions to create doubt in your mind and heart.

The Enemy's tactics and strategies were revealed in the book of Genesis thousands of years ago, and his ways have not changed. Jesus said, "In this world you will have trouble." We see that truth through the millions of babies aborted every year right here in the United States. We see that truth in the countless murders, assaults, divorces, suicides, overdoses, and so much more. Fortunately, Jesus didn't stop there. He added, "But take heart! I have overcome the world" (John 16:33). Why would he say that? Because he wanted us to know that the ultimate battle is already won, which means that we, too, are overcomers in this world. "Jesus Christ is the same yesterday and today and forever" (Hebrews 13:8). Unmask the real Enemy in your marriage, and expose him and his strategies so that you are better equipped to fight.

Selfishness Steals the Joy of Marriage

Kathy and I always had a power struggle about who controlled our finances—it was one of those ways in which we viewed each other as the enemy. Kathy wanted me to follow her rules on how and when to spend our money, and I tried to buy what I wanted and manage our money my way. As much as she tried, Kathy couldn't force me to conform to what I considered to be a tight, structured, and budgeted lifestyle, or as she called it, "being responsible." Ultimately, it would take an act of God to change my heart and thinking.

Spending money was one of my coping strategies, a way to numb the unaddressed pain in my life, and I wasn't going to give it up without a fight. It was selfish, and selfishness, well, it robs you. It's a thief, a weapon deployed by the Enemy to destroy you. Spending money was something that mattered to me more than it should have. That meant it had a priority spot in my heart. Jesus said, "Where your treasure is, there your heart will be also" (Matthew 6:21). My treasure was in buying whatever I wanted whenever I wanted it, even if it meant going into debt. Even if it robbed me of peace and created disunity in my marriage.

God teaches us through his Word. But sometimes we heed the message only after we have fallen flat on our faces. And that's what we did. The only thing more frustrating than not being on the same financial page as Kathy was lacking money, not only for the new things I wanted but also for the old things we had bought on credit.

As with so many other times in my life, it wasn't until I hit a wall that I finally surrendered and God allowed me another chance to do things his way.

Maybe you can relate. A treasure is anything we value

to the point that we're willing to fight for it, to defend our right to have it, even when it hurts those around us. Perhaps your treasure is in feeling good, being successful, or getting attention and recognition. Whatever it is, if your treasure is not pleasing to God, you will never have the peace and joy God intended you to have. Like me, you may have chosen to do a one-eighty from his direction only to find yourself in another mess, wondering, *Why do I always have to learn things the hard way?*

Looking back, it's now very clear why I had to take the long and bumpy road to doing things his way. I didn't want to take that long road, but I had so much to learn. I wanted a shortcut, a quick path to having everything I wanted. I didn't want to wait and work for things. I wanted them all *now*.

Ironically, I taught my MMA and Brazilian jiu-jitsu students just the opposite. I even hung a poster at the front of my school with a picture of some stairs. The first step was a white belt, then came blue, purple, and brown belts; at the top was a black belt. The headline on the poster read: "The elevator to success is out of order. You'll have to take the stairs." In other words, there are no shortcuts in this world. For things we value in life, we need to work hard. We have to invest our time and wait before we can enjoy the fruits of our labor. That is why the things we earn the long and hard way are often the things we value most in our lives.

Part of my issue with selfishness was that even in my lowest moments, I struggled with seeing myself as greedy or selfish. I liked to think of myself as a "give you the shirt off my back" kind of guy. However, as I look back, it's clear that the one thing that kept me from having the marriage God intended was my selfishness. Ultimately, that was what led Kathy and me in different directions financially. There were many instances when I knew I was making poor financial choices. I had a clear intuition from God as he was raising up red flags, but I still wanted my stuff *now*. I had to have granite countertops, an eight-foot-deep pool, a hot tub, a built-in grill, and a new Jeep. The list went on and on.

When Kathy resisted and tried to do the right thing for us, I asserted my authority as the "breadwinner." I put my foot down and reasoned that I deserved what I wanted because I worked hard. Sadly, short-term selfish gain never satisfies. The new car smell doesn't last, the pool becomes a maintenance nightmare, and the granite countertops are covered with more and more bills. Eventually, Kathy gave up the fight to gain some peace. And at that point, I actually thought I'd won!

After all this selfish behavior, there was a defining moment when God changed my view on finances. When I hit rock bottom, I finally made the choice to be the man God created me to be and took an inventory of my life, including my finances. That's when God convicted me that my view of money and possessions was all wrong. In my emptiness, I had again attempted to fill a hole in my heart that only God could fill.

Once I began to have a biblical understanding of money and possessions and discover the life and purpose God had for me, my selfish desires began to abate. Instead of wanting to live for myself, I found a calling to live for and to serve others. This led to a new way of thinking that changed my life. I started to view money as a tool I could use to invest in others rather than something to selfishly spend on myself. Kathy and I were just beginning the Mighty Oaks Foundation, our ministry to veterans and their families, and I began to understand the impact we were having. I could truly see the power our financial resources had to save lives, to change a family's legacy, to make an impact for eternity. In the past I had viewed money in terms of things I could purchase, but now I began to view money from the perspective of a servant's heart.

I learned to see money as a tool not only to provide for my family but also to finance the ministry to which God had called me. This new way of thinking immediately became a new way of living. I still sometimes feel tempted to buy things I don't really need, but each time I make one of those irresponsible purchases, I inevitably regret it and gain an even deeper desire to be more responsible with the resources God has entrusted to me.

As I look back, I was never really happy with or felt fulfilled by my free-spending lifestyle. Yet I feel complete contentment now. My family has everything they need, and we are nearly debt free. Today, we save in advance to pay for things we want, instead of relying on credit cards. What a concept! This new financial approach is not something I would have done in response to Kathy's pleas. This is a choice I made. I chose to be on the same financial page as my wife. Our unity was not achieved because we decided to do things her way or mine, but because we sought out and discovered God's way. His way truly satisfies the desires of our hearts and keeps us in unity.

How do you defeat selfishness in marriage? You choose selfless service. Simply put: you consider your spouse before yourself. You place the desires, wishes, and needs of your spouse before your own. If you must fight, remember who the real Enemy is, and fight to prefer your spouse over yourself. When spouses are consistently selfless, they position themselves for healthier and more fulfilling marriages.

Selfishness is an Enemy tactic. It will destroy your relationships. It will rob you of joy. It will kill intimacy and passion in your marriage. There is no doubt. I appreciate the words of Dennis and Barbara Rainey with FamilyLife, who say that surrender is key in defeating selfishness.[1] Marriage is not an opportunity to amplify selfishness by insisting on doing things our way. Rather, it is a prime opportunity to team up as husband and wife to defeat selfishness and show our children and those around us the power of selfless love. That is how Jesus loves us—selflessly. And that is how we are to operate within marriage.

Pride Kills the Growth of Your Marriage

Earlier in my life, I approved of me a lot more than others approved of me. I was happy with my life and the way I lived.

But that led to a life of sin, because happiness isn't holiness. If I had made a habit of patting myself on the back every time I did something well as a marine, someone would have called me out on it, probably sooner than later. And you don't raise your own hand when you win an MMA fight. The referee does it. Why? Because otherwise every fighter would declare themselves the winner!

Self-approval is smug, and there's a word for that. It's called pride.

When pride is in charge, we don't see where we need to grow, and so we become complacent. And while we're spending all our time polishing our trophies, pride wolfishly creeps at the doorstep. Pride says, "Hey, you're a good person, so one drink isn't going to hurt," or "Just watching one quick video to get the juices flowing isn't a big deal." Or maybe it's one smoke, one line, one text, one visit. Pride tells you you're above it all, that nothing can touch you—until it does. That's when one drink turns into alcoholism, one video becomes a pornography addiction, and so on.

Pride is an Enemy tactic based on self-deception. Think about it. Satan didn't tempt Adam and Eve with a blatant sin, right? Instead, Satan used subtle suggestions to create doubt in their minds that caused them to question God's goodness. We've given the Enemy entirely too much margin to run in our lives. The boundaries we set for our spouses are often narrower than the boundaries we give Satan in our minds, hearts, and lives. That's why pride is a silent killer, a lethal sniper unseen until it is too late.

The effects of pride are much like putting a frog in a pot of warm water and slowly increasing the heat until the frog is in a full boil. Too late. Too much heat to jump out! Eventually, pride will lead to loneliness, bitterness, and, quite possibly worst of all, indifference. Sometimes the symptom of pride looks a lot like complacency. It so slowly affects your sensibilities that you don't realize it until you or your marriage is nearly totally destroyed from within.

How can you defeat pride and prevent it from killing the growth in your marriage? By being intentional and consistent in actively seeking out ways to grow individually and as a couple. Together, you can beat this silent killer. Be active and present in your marriage. Be intentional about demonstrating the love your spouse needs in the way they need it. Remember, pride is subtle but invasive. That means you cannot—absolutely cannot—surrender any ground to the Enemy when it comes to pride. What you are willing to tolerate or justify will eventually dominate you if you let it.

Here are four essential and proven strategies to help you overcome pride in your marriage:

1. *Set shared goals.* Set goals you can work on and accomplish together. Maybe it is a fitness goal, a hobby, or a dream you want to achieve. Having a shared goal is a reminder that you cannot accomplish every goal alone, and that will help to keep your pride in check.

2. *Be spontaneous.* Routines are good, but sometimes it's also good to break up the monotony. Be spontaneous with gestures of love, trips, special dates, and sex. This is a good way to let pride know it doesn't run your life.

3. *Unplug.* Seriously, turn off your devices. The email and text messages can wait. Unplug and spend time together face-to-face. Enjoy the undistracted intimacy technology has stolen from so many couples.

4. *Grow together.* Football coach Lou Holtz once said, "There's a fact in life: you are either growing or you are dying."[2] Choose to grow together. You can do this through marriage counseling or a marriage class, online or in person. Do this through effective and healthy communication and being intentional about keeping complacency in check.

There's no doubt the Enemy will use pride as a tactic to make you complacent and undermine your marriage. But you can fight him together by fighting for each other and developing a strategic battle plan.

Develop Your Strategy

To be intentional with your devotion to Christ and to each other, you need a plan, a strategy, one you can execute every day for the long haul. Anyone can do the work necessary for a day, maybe even a week. But consistency is king, and if you want the rewards of a thriving marriage, you need to be consistent in your efforts and execution of the plan.

To create a plan, you will need to commit to these key elements:

- Acknowledge your marriage must be based on your relationship with Christ. Without him at the center, you will fail.
- Create a daily spiritual discipline of regular Bible study and prayer. Make time for it.
- Pray together daily. It is incredibly difficult to stay angry with your spouse while holding hands in prayer.
- Recognize there is an Enemy who wants to destroy your marriage, and that his mission is to kill, steal, and destroy. He often begins with creating division.
- Discuss the areas where external or internal conflict is attempting to create division in your marriage.
- Write a daily note to your spouse based on Scripture. Be consistent.
- Keep a keen eye out for symptoms of complacency and selfishness in your marriage.

Remember, you are a team, a unit assigned to fight for each other, not against each other. The missions or challenges you face in this life will require you to have a united front. Now is your opportunity to begin doing just that. Create a plan for defeating selfishness and pride when they arise. You have the tools and the knowledge to avoid falling victim to complacency. You are one step closer to having a marriage that can withstand the battles of this life. But you must equip yourself. No one else is going to do the work God has equipped and called you to do in your marriage.

While you have an Enemy who wants to destroy your marriage, there is also a champion present. When your marriage is centered on Christ, you are both champions in Christ. You are more than conquerors over the Enemy of your soul. You do not battle alone, even when you feel alone. With the tools you have now, it is time to execute the plan! Doing so will require consistency, discipline, and time. Preparation without execution is not good stewardship of the tools you have acquired. Put into practice what you have learned.

DISCUSSION

- As you look back over your marriage, when would you say you fell victim to complacency? What were the warning signs, and how did you respond?
- In what ways has the Enemy used selfishness and pride to undermine your marriage in the past and recently?
- Briefly review the four strategies for overcoming pride in your marriage (pages 71–72). Which strategy would most benefit your marriage right now?

AFFIRMATION

We serve a God of love. He does not change. The battles of this life will require us to depend on him to be our strength and on his presence to be our guide. We claim the promise that God's mercies are new every morning (Lamentations 3:22–23), and we shake off any complacency and repent of any selfishness. We are selfless lovers, and we actively pursue Jesus and each other. We fight for each other.

ACTION

- Set a time to pray for your spouse every day. This is one way to break out of spiritual complacency in your marriage.
- Think of one way you can serve your spouse this week and do it with joy and love. The only way to defeat selfishness in your marriage is to actively and consistently serve your spouse selflessly. Service is the antidote to selfishness.
- Be on the lookout for one way pride may be seeping into your heart and mind. Write it down and submit it to God, asking him to help you overcome it and to lead your marriage to Christ.

ROUND III

ACCEPT THAT YOU CAN'T CHANGE THE EVILS YOU'VE ENCOUNTERED

CHAPTER 5

Overcoming Evil

DURING ONE OF MY AFGHANISTAN DEPLOY-
ments, a teammate and I were enjoying some long overdue
downtime by picking up a few essentials from Chicken
Street, a popular marketplace in Kabul that both locals
and foreigners visit for groceries or souvenirs. While it is a
popular marketplace for locals and foreigners, it is *not* an
epicenter of five-star resorts. It is a prime location for the
Taliban to commit terrorist attacks on the patrons going
about their days.

While we were there, we were approached by a young
girl who will be forever known to me as the Girl on Chicken
Street. She and her sister were selling maps and newspapers
published in a mix of English and Dari, the local dialect of
Kabul. After a brief exchange with the girls, we finished our
shopping and walked about a block away when we heard the
concussive sound of an explosion. We looked back to where

we had just been and saw debris and dust still flying through the air as people screamed and ran away.

In the aftermath, we learned that soldiers had been wounded and two children had been killed, one of whom was our little friend. One of our team members said a Chechen suicide bomber with a string of hand grenades attached to his body had located a few Afghan National Army soldiers on a security patrol and self-detonated to kill them. The girl and her sister had been trying to earn enough money that day just to survive, when she was murdered. The vivid memory of the Girl on Chicken Street haunts me to this day, an example of the trauma that plagues both military service members and first responders when they encounter evil up close.

Even if you've never experienced violent conflict, you no doubt bear your own scars and wounds from encounters with the evil of this world. Having scars from past battles is not an indication that you have been overcome by evil; it is a reminder that you are a vulnerable human being living in a fallen world. It also means that you carry those scars and wounds into your relationships, including marriage.

One common challenge for marriages is the issues one or both spouses bring into the relationship, including various forms of past trauma. Therefore, we must clearly identify and look for the symptoms of evil when we are overcome by it. In the pages that follow, both Kathy and I will share the issues we brought into our marriage, and how we pursued forgiveness, reconciliation, and healing.

One of the first things we did was deal with our "baggage." Specifically, we needed to get rid of the unnecessary burdens we were carrying from past trauma. That's something every couple has to do, because we all have baggage of one kind or another. For example, a study published in 2018 revealed that more than 60 percent of the American adults surveyed had at least one adverse childhood experience, and nearly a quarter reported having three or more.[1]

Think about it like this: if you're going to make an arduous climb to the peak of a mountain, you need to take only the tools and resources that are necessary, not things that will weigh you down. In marriage, this means emptying baggage and addressing toxic and evil things from your past and present so you can climb higher together in your relationship.

What Are You Carrying?

Kathy and I both come from broken homes, and we each brought a fair amount of baggage into our marriage. We went into adulthood looking for the fulfillment we missed out on in childhood and adolescence. Kathy had a deep desire to feel loved, to be rescued, and to be taken to a safe place. She needed an environment that offered security, and she wanted assurance that I would never abandon her. Unfortunately, I couldn't meet those needs without first identifying what I was missing in my life, the void I longed to fill.

I came into our marriage carrying both a deep sense of rejection and the pain of losing my teenage brother. In the early years of our marriage, I took the easy way out. I blamed the hardships of life—from my childhood to my deployments in Afghanistan—for who I had become. It wasn't until I began the journey of discovering God's love that I was able to come to terms with the evil I had encountered. God's love is what enabled both Kathy and me to discover the only source that could truly meet our needs and heal our wounds: a personal relationship with Jesus.

When it goes unaddressed, childhood trauma, like war-related trauma, can lead to several issues in our lives. Maybe you have unaddressed trauma from your past, and the toil of carrying those traumas is having a negative effect on your life and your relationships. Often these issues include feeling detached from family or friends, negative thoughts about yourself or others, hopelessness about your future, memory problems, and addiction, to name a few.[2]

What symptoms of trauma do you see in yourself? Look deep inside your bag. It's vital to identify these issues in your heart because your heart carries the deepest wounds.

Kathy:

I felt completely hopeless as I stood in the shower, my face bathed with water and tears. Chad and I had just separated, and I could not see anything but pain in my family's future. "Why is this happening to me?" I cried out audibly to God. "Help me! I can't do this. I need you.

I can't be strong on my own." I wasn't angry with God, but I was mentally and emotionally exhausted. I wanted him to free me from the nightmare I was living in the aftermath of Chad's choices. My soul needed rest.

When we choose to come to Jesus, we find rest in him. He joins himself to us and helps us learn a better way to live. Jesus didn't say, "Come to me and there will be no yoke or burden." He said, "Take my yoke upon you and learn from me" (Matthew 11:29). In other words, "Yoke yourself to me. I'll help you shoulder your burden and teach you how to live." When we yoke ourselves to Jesus and take on only what he has for us, we have access to the divine strength we need even to walk through what the Bible calls the "valley of the shadow of death" (Psalm 23:4 NKJV).

Jesus warned us that "in this world [we] will have trouble" (John 16:33). But we can have peace in the midst of that trouble, because Jesus overcame the greatest of all evils and will help us to overcome whatever we are facing. When we take our burdens to him, he lightens our load through the provision of his peace. His path is one that relieves us of *our* burdens. His burden is much lighter, and he gives us strength in life's battles, which through him are already won. Eliminate these burdens today by first acknowledging they exist and bringing them before God.

As a couple, you may face seasons of overwhelming stress, but you do not have to carry your burdens alone. Jesus is in the battle with you both! The same God who stood with every hero in the Bible invites you to bring your burdens to him. Once you experience his peace and strength, you will want to make a practice of surrendering those burdens to God daily through prayer, knowing you were never created to carry those burdens on your own. Empty your baggage of past evil, lighten the load, and get prepared to address your present reality.

Chad:

I was stunned when I opened the envelope with divorce papers from Kathy. My life had been on a hopeless path, but the looming finality of divorce accelerated my descent. I came very close to taking my own life, and only later I learned that relationship problems are a contributing factor for 42 percent of those who die by suicide.[3] My turning point came when Kathy hit me with the question, "Why don't you *fight for us*?" That's when the change happened.

Selfishness had led me down a tumultuous and damaging path, as it will any man or woman who surrenders to it. Until that point in my life, I was a "maybe I do" husband but an all-in marine and MMA fighter. After Kathy served me divorce papers, I had to decide if I was going to continue to be a "maybe I do" husband and end up divorced and broken, or if I was going to go all in with no more backup plans, no more plan Bs. It required 100 percent commitment and a realignment of my heart and priorities. As a couple, we had to get to a place where we eliminated all secondary plans and exit strategies. Instead of fights between us, we had to learn how to fight for us.

It was never Kathy's job to "fix" me in my sinful state or to heal me when I was diagnosed with PTSD. In fact, she never tried to do either. She supported me and loved me, even when she reached her own breaking point. Although she didn't know it at the time, research has shown that demanding behavioral changes from a spouse seldom leads to any positive outcomes. As three psychology professors wrote in their book *Reconcilable Differences*, "People cannot change their basic essence even if they try to do so. Whether or not it is morally wrong for partners to press for change, it is futile to do so."[4]

Your heart is vulnerable and needs to be guarded with care. How would you guard your home if you knew intruders were coming to cause you or your family harm? You would do so with relentless vigilance, right? And yet, even though we know we have an Enemy, too many of us leave our hearts vulnerable to attack, and the harvest of evil seeds isn't seen until years later. We need to heed the wisdom of Scripture, which reminds us, "Above all else, guard your heart, for everything you do flows from it" (Proverbs 4:23). It is our responsibility to guard our hearts.

Think about it like this: your travel bag has limited capacity, so you focus on packing just what you need and what will fit in your bag. You don't need your entire wardrobe or every book you own for a weekend trip. It would be foolish to attempt to pack a car engine, a kitchen sink, a king-size bed, or some other odd object. In much the same way, your heart also has limited capacity. Your heart can only carry so much, and if it's full of unprocessed trauma, your life and relationships are going to be overburdened and messy. If you store up good things in your heart, good things will flow from it. But if you allow the evil from your past to take the throne of your heart, you will reap the fruits of evil.

Here's the good news: we *do* have a choice about what we allow to take up residence in our hearts. When we take the trauma of our pasts seriously and decide to deal with it rather than deny it or avoid it, we effectively issue a notice of eviction to those remnants of past evils in our lives. It's time to let go of the past by facing up to it. The longer we allow it to take up space in our hearts, the more our quality of life and our relationships will suffer.

This kind of healing is a process and is seldom instantaneous. However, all that is required of you now is to take the next best step. It might be simply acknowledging how far you have come, having a conversation with your spouse about your healing journey, or working with a pastor, counselor, or mentor to help you. Don't be a hoarder of negative experiences from your past. Instead, open your heart, your hands, and your life to the healing power of God.

When I think of emptying my baggage, this invitation from Jesus comes to mind:

Come to me, all you who are weary and burdened, and I
will give you rest. Take my yoke upon you and learn from
me, for I am gentle and humble in heart, and you will find
rest for your souls. For my yoke is easy and my burden is
light. (Matthew 11:28–30)

Don't try to fix your spouse, whether it's their present
behavior or the legacy of past experiences. Your best hope
for dealing with any present evils within your marriage is to
be present—to be a listening and supportive ear, to validate
emotions, and to get professional help individually and as a
couple when needed.

Commenting on the impact of past trauma on marriage, Amy Bushatz, a military spouse and executive editor
at Military.com, wrote, "It's normal for PTSD to impact the
whole family," so that even when you're not the one suffering
from PTSD, "you may have symptoms anyway."[5] This may
be your present reality due to current circumstances or past
trauma, but it does not have to determine your future.

Be the one who initiates a discussion about the power
of God's love, or better yet, who demonstrates that love in
a tangible way. One of the best things you can do in marriage when your partner is suffering from past trauma is to
demonstrate love, extend grace, and forgive frequently. I will
say it again: it is not your job to fix your spouse. God will
give you the power to love, stand with, and support your
spouse—and to get professional help when needed.

Instead of demanding that your spouse change, try the conciliatory approach described by the apostle Paul, "Submit to one another out of reverence for Christ" (Ephesians 5:21). Demanding change leads to conflict, but humbly submitting to each other out of reverence for Christ leads to peace. Submitting to each other does not mean tolerating abuse or being a doormat. The humble submission that comes out of reverence for Christ is a choice, which means it is a decision made from a position of power. You have the power to release resentment, surrender grudges, and practice forgiveness. Those are not options for the weak. This conciliatory approach is driven by love and only possible when two people are willing to walk by the Spirit of God. (An important note: if you are presently in an abusive relationship, seek trusted professional help immediately. This book alone is not an adequate resource to guide you through this situation.)

Kathy recognized I needed help. I will be forever grateful for the challenge she presented to me in that apartment. But there are some situations where the best way we can show grace is to seek trusted professional help, again, especially if there is abuse present. Please don't take how Kathy handled our situation as a permission slip to remain in dangerous situations. Sometimes God gives us grace to address a situation head-on, and sometimes his grace leads us to safety in another direction.

The grace and love Kathy showed me became a powerful revelation of God's unconditional love for me. It's unlikely that would have happened if she had issued ultimatums and demanded change. Instead, she loved me as Jesus does. I now know it was the power of God that was working through Kathy to get my attention.

You are not alone in your fight against the legacy of trauma in your life. God stands with you—and nothing is impossible when God's power is at work in a marriage. When you focus on who he is to you and what he is to your marriage, you shift your focus from the challenges you face to gratitude for all God has done and is going to do.

The psalmist proclaimed God's faithfulness to those who cried out to him when they were suffering:

> Then they cried to the LORD in their trouble,
> > and he saved them from their distress.
> He brought them out of darkness, the utter
> darkness,
> > and broke away their chains.
> Let them give thanks to the LORD for his
> unfailing love
> > and his wonderful deeds for mankind,
> for he breaks down gates of bronze
> > and cuts through bars of iron.
> (Psalm 107:13–16)

The strongest bars may be holding you both prisoner in your present reality, but by his power and through his love,

God will break down those walls, shatter the prison doors, and deliver you from distress. God helped Kathy and I find this freedom.

Kathy:

After crying out desperately to God in the shower that day, I began to pray for Chad. Not because I wanted to (How do you pray for someone you don't like?), but because I felt the Lord was asking me to. I also wanted to be set free of the hate I had toward him. I didn't want our kids to see hate between Chad and me the way I had witnessed it in my divorced parents.

My "change him" plan had turned into a "change me" plan. My prayer was now: *Change my heart, God, and let me see Chad the way you see him. Let me love Chad the way you love him. And let me forgive Chad the way you forgive him.*

At the time, Chad and I were still preparing for our impending divorce. But as I faithfully trusted God to help get me through the pain, he gave me the ability to begin forgiving Chad. I would never have been able to truly forgive Chad without humbling myself first and accepting my own faults for our failing marriage. I was not being naive or justifying Chad's actions but merely accepting my part, because I had not been the wife that God had called me to be since I had not truly forgiven Chad.

Chad:

My father was a marine Vietnam veteran and dealt with many of the same issues our troops bring home from combat in modern wars. He was a violent man when I was growing up, and that created a lot of bitterness in my heart toward him. Before Kathy and I launched the Mighty Oaks Foundation, there was a ten-year period in which I heard from my dad only when he needed money. I held a deep and resentful anger toward him for many reasons. It was during this ten-year period that I went into my downward spiral, and it nearly destroyed our marriage. But through Kathy, I experienced the grace and love of God. She was the vessel God used to show me his love in human form. As a result, I was eventually deeply convicted in my heart about the hate I had harbored toward my dad.

We launched the Mighty Oaks Foundation in 2011, and about a month later, I received a call from a hospital nurse saying I was the only next-of-kin listed for my father. She said he was on life support and they needed my involvement. I was extremely angry and wanted nothing to do with him. But when I took some time to reflect on that call, the only thing I could think of was the love and forgiveness I had experienced from Kathy and how God had been changing me through a second chance I didn't deserve. In fact, I concluded that what my dad had done to me wasn't remotely close to all the damage I had done to others in my life—to Kathy, family, friends, and especially toward God. Who was I to withhold the same forgiveness from my dad that so many others had offered to me?

Before my dad passed away, I had the opportunity to experience a restored relationship with him and was blessed to lead him to Christ. There were still difficult times, but I heard him say multiple times, "I love you, Chad, and I am so sorry," in the days leading up to his death. Forgiveness is not something you will regret on your deathbed, unless you withhold it.

Maybe your marriage is in a place where forgiveness hasn't been a practice and you now experience resentment and contempt for each other. When you consistently withhold forgiveness from your spouse, it won't be long until it becomes impossible to forgive. The times when forgiveness is easy aren't the times when forgiveness matters most. That was one of my greatest lessons, and it was one of Kathy's best gifts to me. She chose to forgive me when it was hard. She taught me that forgiveness was the answer even when I did not change or when her efforts had no immediate impact on my behavior. When it came to forgiving my dad, I didn't immediately feel differently, and he didn't immediately change. It was a process that began with my choice to forgive and to let go of my hard feelings toward him. I will forever be grateful to Kathy for showing me how to forgive by forgiving me.

Unforgiveness is deadly. Within marriage, it creates room for the evil done against us to become bitterness, resentment, and emotional distance. And that is essentially what unforgiveness is: holding on to the evil thing that has happened until we get what we consider justice. True forgiveness looks at evil square in the face, acknowledges what it is and the destruction it has caused, then surrenders it into God's care, trusting that he will make things right in his way and in his timing.

Given the amount of research on forgiveness in recent years, it is important to note the proven benefits of forgiveness pertaining to marriage.[6] Forgiveness is not weakness. Forgiveness is not condoning the behavior of the offender. Forgiveness is a decision to release resentment and vengeance so you can move on from the past and embrace a better future. Theologian Lewis Smedes wrote, "To forgive is to set a prisoner free and discover that the prisoner was you."[7]

Terry Gaspard, a therapist with the Gottman Institute, encourages couples to "think like a forgiving person."[8] In other words, refuse to hold a grudge and be quick to extend compassion. Take baby steps in addressing each other's offenses and do it *daily*. Don't allow emotional and relational wounds to fester into deeper issues. Instead, address them promptly and directly. The apostle Paul wrote, "Be kind and compassionate to one another, forgiving each other, just as in Christ God forgave you" (Ephesians 4:32). Remember that the Father sees you and your spouse *through* his Son, Jesus. He sees you with eyes of compassion, washed completely clean because of Jesus' death and resurrection.

Demonstrating compassion and forgiveness toward your spouse is a powerful and effective weapon for overcoming evil together. Practicing forgiveness when it matters most will never be easy, but it will set you free and shine the light of heaven on your marriage.

After Forgiveness

The grace Kathy showed me caused me to take immediate action, which ultimately led me to surrender my life to Christ and to learn to forgive myself.

After we forgive, we must begin moving our lives closer to Christ and living according to his Word. We cannot forgive and continue with our sinful behavior. The greatest action we can take is to recommit our lives to God and to each other. Implement the lessons in this book on a consistent and daily basis. Not for ten days, two months, or a year, but for a lifetime. Then the anchor of your story is no longer pain, but hope. When we take the proper steps after forgiveness, hope is born. Our marriages can be reconciled, and new life can blossom.

Forgiveness requires humility because it is a form of letting go. When you forgive, you relinquish your offender into the hands of God. Forgiving yourself or others as an act of faith and out of obedience to God requires taking a step closer to Christ, and this is one of the most beneficial actions you can take as a couple. Being quick to forgive, knowing you may not immediately feel differently about the situation, and being consistent in forgiving will produce tremendous joy and freedom. You may never forget the offense, but you can relinquish your resentment and bitterness to God in exchange for peace and joy.

DISCUSSION

- In speaking about marriage, Jesus said, "What God has joined together, let no one separate" (Mark 10:9). In what ways has a past evil been getting in the way of your relationship with God or your spouse?
- What present evils or sins do you need to guard your heart against? Consider your own sinful tendencies and behaviors as well as evil you face in this world.
- In what ways have you experienced or witnessed the power of forgiveness? How might practicing forgiveness help you to overcome evil as a couple?

AFFIRMATION

We claim the promise that God can make all things new in our marriage. We refuse to allow the evils we've encountered to dictate our joy, our peace, or the health of our marriage. We are resilient, and we forge ahead in God's strength and power. We are more than conquerors through Jesus, and we will overcome evil with good. We commit to forgiving each other and continuing to love each other as God strengthens our marriage.

ACTION

- When you see evil at work, name it. Say to each other, "Our Enemy is the evil, not each other." Then join forces to fight the evil together.
- Identify and acknowledge the ways you've sinned against each other and practice forgiveness. Follow these steps:

For the person who has sinned
› Verbalize to God and your spouse your sorrow for what you have done.
› Admit you were wrong and express your desire to act differently.
› Ask God and your spouse to forgive you.
› Be patient and understand that forgiveness isn't always instantaneous; sometimes it is a process.

For the person who has been sinned against
› Ask God to show you how he sees your spouse.
› Listen to your spouse's heart, even if the words are not exactly what you hope to hear.
› Say "I love you, and I forgive you," or "I love you, and I am willing to forgive you, but I'm not there yet."

For both of you

› Give your situation to God and ask for his help—daily.

› Discuss how you want to respond to this issue if it comes around again.

- Consider making the act of forgiveness more tangible through an external representation of what you're doing in your heart. You could write down the burden, debt, or evil you have forgiven on slips of paper. Place each one in a jar to symbolize that you are giving them to God. If hard feelings surface, surrender them to God. Ask him for the strength you need to leave that issue in his hands, and trust him to make it right in his way and in his time.

CHAPTER 6

LIFE PIVOT

WINSTON CHURCHILL, PARAPHRASING JOHN Henry Newman, once said, "To improve is to change, so to be perfect is to have changed often."[1] Change is inevitable in life, and some changes cannot be avoided. But to willingly surrender our will to the perfect will of God for our lives, well, it's not easy. It is, however, worth the effort.

Serving in the Marine Corps not only exposed me to a whole new way of life, but it also gave me a new vocabulary, even for the simplest things. For example, in the Marine Corps a bathroom is the *head*. A window is a *porthole*. A door is a *hatch*. Running shoes are *go-fasters*. A flashlight is a *moon beam*. And when you're walking, you don't turn, you *pivot*—and you do it sharply and quickly at a perfect ninety-degree angle.

To pivot is to make a decisive change in direction. That's why organizations often use the word *pivot* to describe changes in strategy or policy. Sometimes pivots are proactive, but sometimes they happen in response to unexpected circumstances or failures—when the need for change is undeniable. When something doesn't go successfully on a military operation, it often leads to new policy developments, rules, guidelines, and standard operating procedures. Throughout American history, amazing stories of military heroes who have had to pivot due to challenging situations and changing circumstances—sometimes after they have served our country—remind us of how important this trait is.

I've had to make a few pivots in my life, and I'm guessing you have too. Change begins with small adjustments, and maybe like someone serving in the US Armed Forces, today is the mark, the point of your pivot, where you begin to make the necessary changes to ensure positive outcomes in your marriage.

When I had come to a very clear point in my life where everything I had tried wasn't working, I finally realized it was time to try something different. In my own life and when I counsel others, I ask, "If what you're doing isn't working, then why not try something different?" Maybe it's time to pivot.

How smooth that transition is depends on multiple factors, including your circumstances, season of life, and how well prepared you are to make a change. Life pivots are rarely easy or pleasant. For example, deciding to pivot from a self-centered life to a selfless life doesn't instantly free you from the consequences of past behavior, and it doesn't erase the memory of what you did or what happened to you. Instead, pivoting means you are in the process of changing your direction, of leaving the past behind and straining toward the good that lies ahead.

Pressing on to a New Vision

When you pivot in marriage, you make a decision as a couple to leave the past behind and press on toward your future together. You choose to align your life and marriage with the good intentions of God. You turn away from the past so you can turn toward a new vision. If your entire field of view is focused on the past, there is no room for that vision—and it is a sure way to stunt the growth of or even destroy your marriage.

If you've ever thought, *It doesn't have to be this way; there has to be something better,* you are correct. The apostle Paul acknowledged his own pivot—to leave the past behind and focus on a vision of the future—when he wrote:

> Not that I have already obtained all this, or have already arrived at my goal, but I press on to take hold of that for which Christ Jesus took hold of me. Brothers and sisters, I do not consider myself yet to have taken hold of it. But one thing I do: Forgetting what is behind and straining toward what is ahead, I press on toward the goal to win

the prize for which God has called me heavenward in Christ Jesus. (Philippians 3:12–14)

Paul admitted he hadn't yet achieved his goal; he was still in the process. So his statement that he was "forgetting what is behind" suggests he was still aware of the past, that there were still negative memories lingering. If Paul had to work daily to forget the past while simultaneously striving toward what God had planned for him in the future, then we can consider ourselves in good company as we do the same. Paul showed us that we don't have to be stuck in the past. But it requires that we press on with great effort.

Nowhere did Paul say, "Just hang out and be comfortable while the future comes to you." No, pivoting is a decision backed up by hard work, and every pivot is different. Your pivot point might be changing your mindset about your marriage, forgiving your spouse, or facing up to the painful legacies of your past. Whatever it is, shifting your vision from the past to the future is essential.

My biggest pivot point came when I hit rock bottom, when I tried to take my own life, and when I realized I was fighting for all the wrong things. Pain often creates a tunnel vision effect, and all we can focus on is the point of pain. When we do that, we miss out on the potential for pivoting into God's promises. That's the beauty of this life pivot I experienced and what so many others have experienced. It was only when I pivoted from my pain to God's promises that Kathy and I were propelled toward the future God had for us. At the point of our greatest pain, Kathy and I realized we could no longer put off making the changes necessary to save our marriage. We could no longer approach our marriage with the mindset of, *Our marriage will be better when we get our first house, when we have kids, when they go to school, when we retire,* and so on. Our lives would never get better until we pivoted to make them better. Kathy and I chose to adopt the mindset of the apostle Paul—to press on toward the goal and the good future God has for us.

As it was with Paul, we are still in the process. That means making the decision daily to surrender to God's perfect will, discovered through a relationship with his Son, Jesus. For me, pivoting meant allowing Jesus to redeem me, shifting my focus from pain to purpose, and living into my calling to serve others. I was no longer walking in the wrong direction on the wrong path in life. Now I could become the man, the husband, and the father God created me to be.

Relationship Rewards

Relationship with the King of kings is our reward! There is no greater reward than perfect redemption, and through him we discover our purpose. When Kathy and I surrendered to Christ as a couple, we began walking in his promises together.

After you and your spouse make a commitment to live

in his redemption and promises, it's time to dream together. It's time to become one, to lean into your future and press toward what lies ahead as one body.

In the pit of despair, we tend to self-isolate. We often want to go through the pain, the consequences of our sins, alone. We may not be able to escape the earthly consequences of our sins, but Jesus has already paid for our heavenly consequences. There's nothing to strive for; we must only accept his gift, acknowledge it, and receive it into our lives. Nothing we can do, now or ever, will compare to the love Jesus demonstrated for us by giving his life. What is the will of God? That we should live and love our spouses in a way that properly reflects the love he showed us.

In Philippians 3:14, one Greek transliteration of the phrase "to press" means "to pursue." It is impossible to run in two directions at one time. We cannot pursue what is ahead while still holding on to the past. As we pursue a relationship with God, we will be drawn to pursue each other. Whatever may be holding us back from these pursuits must be abandoned. In fact, God's Word promises that as we draw near to him, he will draw near to us. But to draw near to each other, we need mutual effort, consistency, and, yes, patience. These are the keys to experiencing relationship rewards. But without pursuit, the rewards remain unclaimed.

The promises of God are perfect, but we must trust him enough to continue walking through the storm, to continue discovering our purpose through the pain. He will lead us!

The rewards we see as part of our relationship with God mirror the rewards and blessings we receive as a married couple who honor God with our lives. Marriage is meant to be a mirror of how God loves his bride, the church. For a better understanding of this, look at what happened in the garden of Eden, the scene of the most heinous crime in the history of humanity. Satan deceived Eve, and in turn, Eve deceived Adam, and creation was compromised. But now, through God's Son, we have an all-access pass to the throne of God, to the kingdom of God, to a marriage that honors God and leaves a godly legacy for our children.

When we accept this, only then can we begin to shift our focus to what he created us to do and move from trying to manage sin in our own strength to realizing the desire God placed on our hearts to pursue his purpose for our lives, a purpose of serving others. That's what happened to me.

From the beginning of time, God knew his plan for us. It was always a good plan. In Jeremiah 29:11, God spoke to the people of Israel: "'I know the plans I have for you,' declares the LORD, 'plans to prosper you and not to harm you, plans to give you hope and a future.'" God wants to give us a hope and a future, but first we have to surrender to his plans for our lives. He will not force them on us. When we step into a relationship with God for perfect redemption, we also benefit from his promises of a plan and a purpose.

God's Will, Our Purpose

We find our purpose by seeking God's will for our lives. If that seems clear as mud to you, don't worry. When I first learned of this, it was about as clear as mud to me too. The context for this originates in the apostle Paul's statement, "God saved us and called us to live a holy life" (2 Timothy 1:9 NLT). That's our purpose. It means God did not create us for the purpose of being successful in our careers, being famous, gaining a big following on social media, or becoming wealthy. No, we were created and called to be holy.

God has saved us from our sins and called us to a holy life, but we can't live it by our human effort. We are given the strength and wisdom only through the saving grace of God. Yet we have to be willing and ready to follow his call. Maybe you've heard, "If you have to force it, it's not God's will." I believe this is false, a myth, perhaps even bad theology. There are always challenges along the journey; they might even include our mindsets and belief patterns that are out of alignment with God's Word. In a study with the University of Pennsylvania, Larissa Rainey noted, "the vast majority of people crave a sense of purpose in life."[2] When was the last time you tried to pursue the purpose you were certain God created you to fulfill? I knew God's will for me the moment Kathy challenged me. I knew it when I met with Steve Toth. I knew it in the pit of my gut.

One of the best statements I've come across on being aligned with God's will and discovering our purpose is by

Dr. Tony Evans at the Urban Alternative. Dr. Evans wrote, "Moses met God at a burning bush because he came to the mountain where God was hanging out."[3] Moses didn't go to the burning bush because he was looking for his purpose; he went to the burning bush because he was seeking the presence of God. Although I had devoted my life to seeking purpose and fulfillment in everything from serving my country to being a competitive fighter, I hadn't devoted myself to seeking God. In fact, by seeking a purpose instead of seeking God, I effectively idolized my purpose over my relationship with God. Had I made this discovery sooner, I might have saved myself and my family a great deal of pain and heartache.

God is calling us to discover our purpose in our relationship with him by drawing near to his presence as Moses did. Jesus put it this way, "Seek the Kingdom of God above all else, and live righteously, and he will give you everything you need" (Matthew 6:33 NLT). In other words, the kingdom of God must be at the center of our existence. When seeking the kingdom of God is our first priority, we will *want* to abandon our way and surrender to his will—daily. It means that if our lives are centered in him, we effectively have everything we need, and he will reveal to us his will and our purpose. Don't overcomplicate it. He will guide you if you allow him to. Kathy longed for me to lead our home, but it was impossible for me to be an effective leader of my family until I surrendered to the lordship of Christ.

Heart Transformation

Over the years, I have talked to numerous men in our Mighty Oaks programs who are confused about finding God's purpose for them. Often I am asked, "Chad, how can I know God's will for me?" Or, like I recently heard, "It just seems like a fairy tale or fantasy to think God cares enough about me to reveal his purpose and will for my life." My response is to point out that God's will isn't hard to find because God isn't hard to find.

What if I told you I have a secret that will set your life ablaze for goodness and change you forever? Here's the perfect will of God for you, me, and everyone else: to come to know Jesus as Savior. Then, in the words of Billy Graham, "[God] wants you to discover in your daily life what it means to live for Him and follow His will."⁴ The most significant pivot we can make in life begins when we turn away from the pain life has presented to us and pursue the life and love God offers us through his Son, Jesus. When we relinquish the pain and failures of our past, he gives us his best for our lives. When we come into a relationship with our Creator, we begin to live the life we were created to live, and we are even able to share that good news with others. Finding meaning and purpose really is that simple—and that complex.

It's simple because it just requires that we make a decision; it's complex because living out that decision requires ongoing effort and commitment. Our work to serve those who serve through the Mighty Oaks Foundation is a labor of love, and our programs have proven to be incredibly effective on many fronts. But the reality is, humanity doesn't need another program, another church, or another solution. We are at a pivot point in humanity where the single greatest need is a heart transformation, which is something we can't do in our own power.

I can tell you unequivocally that I was a man who had a heart of stone. I lacked empathy and compassion, and I was emotionally numb. That's a dangerous state to be in. But the moment I surrendered to God, he began a good work in me and gave me a new heart. One of my favorite Bible promises is, "I will give you a new heart and put a new spirit in you; I will remove from you your heart of stone and give you a heart of flesh" (Ezekiel 36:26). I can clearly recall the moment when God gave me this new heart and I could feel again. This prayer and moment came after I had surrendered to Christ during my first meeting with Steve Toth.

I sat in my Jeep parked in my driveway and prayed for God to take away the cold bitterness that had consumed my heart. I wanted to feel empathy and compassion once again. I wanted to care about someone besides myself. And you know what? God answered that prayer. As tough as I had been in all the fights and in all the special operation endeavors, at that moment the floodgates of emotion opened, and I wept for hours. Years of suppressed emotion came flooding over me as I cried tears of hurt, regret, and sorrow. Although it was painful to finally feel the hurt I'd caused others, the strongest emotion I felt in that moment was the joy of pivoting, of moving forward with hope in a new direction.

To have a changed heart is the definition of what it means to be in the center of God's will and purpose, because a changed heart changes everything else—our mindset, goals, marriage, relationships, parenting, finances, health, and eternity. Only God can change the human heart, and that change begins when we accept that Jesus paid the price for our sins and our transformation when he died on the cross in our place. Then we commit to our calling when we choose to live a holy life every day by pivoting away from whatever it is that keeps us from moving toward God.

When it comes to your marriage, what prevents you from making a pivot or keeps you from moving toward God? What are you seeking above all else? Most of us tend to prioritize our own pleasure and comfort, so we seek things like money, happiness, security, recognition, or success, instead of seeking first God's kingdom and his righteousness. But none of these things will give us the life or the marriage we want, because they can't lead us closer to God, the source of our purpose. Think about that for a minute. If we never made decisions based on our desire for security and comfort, where would we be? Billions of dollars are spent annually on advertising in our nation because we are incredibly addicted to pleasure, comfort, and convenience.

God's will and purpose for your marriage are for both of you to draw near to him, to seek his kingdom above all else in your relationship. Be selfless in your service to your spouse and commit to surrendering your heart, mind, and will to God daily. This is an essential part of how you fight for your marriage.

More than Rewards

When we make a change, most of us do so because we anticipate an earthly reward. The reward for working out is increased strength and endurance; the reward for studying is a good grade; the reward for practicing piano is a successful recital. However, when it comes to pivoting in life, we have to check our expectations regarding the most beneficial reward, which is a relationship with Jesus.

The harsh reality about making necessary life changes is that it's not about receiving a physical reward or a pat on the back. We will no doubt experience benefits such as peace, healing, and comfort from being in God's will, but we need to make sure our decision to surrender our lives to Jesus isn't transactional. It may be reasonable to consider incentives that help us make some changes, but we must be certain we are not encouraging or developing problematic motivations. Consider the rewards of walking one mile a day with your spouse as a means of improving communication. The primary reward would be an improved marriage, but you'd also improve your physical health. Expecting rewards for behavior changes is not necessarily bad. However, the reward for surrendering our lives to Christ is a rich relationship with our Creator and treasures in heaven (Matthew 6:20). It's not the benefits of life with Christ that change us; it's the relationship with Christ that changes us.

Of course, some changes happen because we're forced to make them. For example, a court orders us to attend anger management classes after we've committed a crime or Alcoholics Anonymous after we've been arrested for driving under the influence of alcohol. These behavior changes aren't voluntary. At these times we need to consider the reasons behind the actions that brought about these consequences.

Authors Donald Miller and Ian Cron once discussed the truth that "to make lasting changes in your life, you need to know the story and themes that run beneath the surface."[5] If your marriage is in a rocky place, then it's time to ask why your marriage began to deteriorate. What's the story? You didn't get married because you hated each other. You married your spouse because you wanted to spend the rest of your lives together. But then "life" happened and there was no time to talk, no time for sex, no time to work on your marriage. If you want to make lasting changes in your marriage, work together to uncover the underlying story behind those pain points. And there *is* time. You're either spending it in a dying marriage or putting in the necessary work to keep your marriage in tip-top shape.

When you choose to pivot, do so because it is the right thing to do and because it's the best thing for you, your marriage, your family, and your future. Make changes because it is what God's Word instructs you to do. After all, it is part of striving for what lies ahead. You are blessed every day you are allowed to serve God and others. But the rewards you are storing up aren't earthly; they aren't rewards you cash in to make yourself more comfortable or successful. These are eternal rewards given to those who serve with pure hearts.

Pivot and Move

The best decision for your life and your marriage begins with an intentional choice to plant yourself where you are and to create a plan and cast a vision for where you are going. Where is your marriage now? Where is God calling you to go? What is your vision for your marriage? The place in which you find yourself may not be a pleasant one. You may be dealing with a painful past, crushing addiction, marital challenges, or financial obstacles. But the biggest life pivots often happen at your points of greatest pain.

Whether your starting point is a consequence of self-defeating habits, an unhealthy lifestyle, or a troubled marriage, you and your spouse can both make a conscious decision today to move in a new and healthier direction. Study the Bible and pray together, and seek professional, godly counsel if necessary. You don't have to pivot alone, nor were you meant to. Focus on what God has called you to do as a couple for his kingdom and move toward that purpose by living a life of holiness.

- How open are you to healthy change in your marriage? Use a scale of one to ten, with one being "not at all open" and ten being "completely open." Share the reasons for the number you chose and discuss whether it may be beneficial to seek the assistance of a Christian counselor.
- If you could pivot to make one change in your marriage, what would it be? How would your life be different if you made this change together?
- In what ways are you intentional about seeking God right now? What pivot decisions might you make to move even closer to God together?
- What is your vision for your marriage?

God did not call us to holiness and then leave us powerless to live a holy life. He has equipped us with the power of the Holy Spirit to guide us, comfort us, and lead us. Through the power of God, we can address the hard places in life and pivot when necessary. To the best of our ability, we commit to leaving the past behind and pressing on toward the good future God has for us.

ACTION

The apostle Paul said, "He has saved us and called us to a holy life—not because of anything we have done but because of his own purpose and grace. This grace was given us in Christ Jesus before the beginning of time" (2 Timothy 1:9). It is by the grace of God and for his own purpose, although we may not recognize it at the time, that we are able to make life pivots at our points of greatest pain. Pivoting is not going to be comfortable at first. But you and your spouse must work together, for each other, to fight through bad decisions, bad habits, addictions—whatever it takes—to strive for a holy life as a couple.

Get specific about what habits you need to break and what habits you need to develop to make this pivot in your marriage. Discuss and write out three bad habits you need to eliminate from your lives and three healthy habits you can commit to building and developing in your lives.

ROUND IV

ACCESS GOD'S POWER

CHAPTER 7

FUEL FOR THE FIGHT

SINCE I WAS THIRTEEN YEARS OLD, I HAVE BEEN running, training, and preparing for a fight. My brother and I made a commitment to each other that we would train and join the Marine Corps to become Recon Marines. Additionally, having been in competitive martial arts since the age of five, it should be no surprise that I'd become a pro MMA fighter. But neither the Marine Corps nor being a professional fighter come without proper training—and there is a *lot* of training involved. All that training must then be paired with proper fuel for your body. It's necessary to put the right amount and the right kind of food in your body to compete at a high level. It's necessary to fuel your body with proper sleep. All the training, proper nutrition, and good sleep would be useless if I had not prepared my heart and mind.

Adam Davis, my brother in Christ and partner in writing

this book, and I have had many conversations about various sports and competitions. During one conversation in particular I realized I don't watch a lot of sports, and that is because I don't believe I was created to be a spectator. I believe I was created to be a participant, a competitor. And competitors know they must have the proper fuel to have a fighting chance to win. It doesn't matter if you are an MMA fighter, an Olympic athlete, or involved in sports at any level, this fuel must be identified and taken.

In retrospect, I had all the tools and the fuel needed to be a marine and a championship-caliber MMA fighter. But when it came to having the fuel to fight for my marriage, my tank was bone dry. I loved competing, I loved to win, and I loved training for every aspect of my military and fighting career. For too long, however, that love was greater than my love for my wife. You see, love fuels us for victory; understanding the love Christ has for us fuels us for victory. If we lack understanding and love, we are not ready to enter the arena of competition.

If you are on a journey to take care of your body, I applaud you. If you are a competitor, my hat is off to you. But you should know there is someone else competing for your heart and the heart of your spouse: the Enemy of your soul. It's time to prepare your heart for battle. It's time to fuel your soul with proper content, specifically from God's Word, so you can be positioned for victory in the arena of battle for your marriage.

We Are Fueled for Victory When We Love

If you're training for a championship fight, you can't load up on junk food and sugary drinks, because you will be at a disadvantage against your opponent who is likely fueling their body with the nutrient-rich foods that build strength and stamina. In the same way, if you're trying to grow individually and as a couple, you can't fuel your mind and heart with the junk food equivalent of movies, music, or other media. Instead, you will need to build strength and stamina with things that will help you fight for your marriage. What fuels every marriage is the nutrient-rich goodness of God's Word and the example set by Jesus for what it means to love each other well.

The apostle Paul gave us a picture of how Jesus loves when he wrote, "Husbands, love your wives, just as Christ loved the church" (Ephesians 5:25). Paul likened Jesus to a soon-to-be-wedded man whose bride is the church. A bridegroom is a man on his wedding day, just before or after the event.[1] Most of the biblical references to a bridegroom refer to Jesus, the perfect Bridegroom. Jesus loves compassionately, unconditionally, and selflessly, and husbands are to love their wives as Jesus loves the church.

It's easy to take Ephesians 5:25 and put the verse on a coffee mug and feel goosebumps. But what does it mean to put this kind of love into practice, to truly love our spouses as Christ loves the church? It requires a mutual submission to Christ as our Lord and to our spouses as we seek to serve each other daily. This submission to Christ as a couple is the foundation for identifying the true Enemy of your soul and your marriage, and for realizing that you and your spouse are not enemies but are on the same team, working as one unit, one flesh, surrendered to Christ.

If we were honest, few of us, if any, have been a good model of the Bridegroom. But when we learn the values of Jesus—that his love is compassionate, unconditional, and selfless—and how he wants us to live out those values, we tap into the source of power we need to remain adequately fueled for the battles of this life, to engage in spiritual warfare, especially when the Enemy wants to undermine our marriage. If we're going to be effective as a married couple in fighting for our marriage, we must be fueled every day by the love and teachings of Jesus. The Bible is our standard operating procedure for spiritual warfare and where we can get the fuel we need for the biggest fight of our lives.

We Are Fueled for Victory When We Live Selflessly

Living selfishly leads to myriad negative consequences in your life, and it creates a plethora of issues in your marriage, including resentment, conflict, and emotional wounds. Selfishness sacrifices the best things of the future for temporary gratification right now. Jesus lived and taught us to do the opposite. We need to look to the way Jesus lived when he physically walked this earth for the power to get through this life. Even though there isn't enough room in this chapter (or this book) to adequately look at the life of Jesus and how he lived, we can get a *glimpse* in a story recorded in Matthew 19.

Jesus had finished teaching and embarked on a journey to Jerusalem from Galilee when he stopped to heal people who were following him. Some Pharisees, a group of religious leaders, took this opportunity to corner Jesus, hoping to entrap him by asking a trick question: "Is it lawful for a man to divorce his wife for any and every reason?" (Matthew 19:3).

The point of debate on which the Pharisees based their question concerned how to interpret Moses' teaching about divorce in Deuteronomy 24:1, 4:

> If a man marries a woman who becomes displeasing to
> him because he finds something indecent about her, and
> he writes her a certificate of divorce . . . that would be
> detestable in the eyes of the LORD.

While some have interpreted the word "indecent" in this verse to mean adulterous behavior, others have considered it to mean anything, however minor, that displeased a husband.[2] At the time, a lax interpretation had led to men abusing the law, and the Pharisees sought to entrap Jesus by forcing him to pick one interpretation or the other.

Instead of falling into the trap, Jesus used Scripture to restate God's original intention for marriage. His response was seasoned with love, grace, and, yes, brutal honesty:

> "Haven't you read," he replied, "that at the beginning the Creator 'made them male and female,' and said, 'For this reason a man will leave his father and mother and be united to his wife, and the two will become one flesh'? So they are no longer two, but one flesh. Therefore what God has joined together, let no one separate." (Matthew 19:4–6)

From the very beginning, God's intention for marriage was that a man and a woman would leave their parents and join together to become "one flesh," one union, until death. Jesus came to empower the body of Christ, the church, you and me, for the battles we face in this life.

Furthermore, we cannot ignore how Jesus responded to these religious teachers when, based on the context of Scripture, he was likely physically tired. His response was polite, compassionate, and loving, proving the importance of not just what we say but also how we say it. There are times when we need to be more intentional about our responses to questions we may deem stupid, especially when we are tired.

And we need to be intentional about taking time to rest, like Jesus did.

We Are Fueled for Victory When We Rest

No warrior wants to enter a battle sleep-deprived. To be victorious in any fight, we need the fuel of proper rest. In his presentations to military and law enforcement audiences, Lt. Col. Dave Grossman often says, "We cannot train our body to get by on less sleep, but what we can do is psychologically empower ourselves. . . . It's critical we prioritize sleep."[3] This means we don't make a habit of denying ourselves the sleep we need to function well.

When it is time for sleep, we sleep. This seems like common sense, right? Yet some of us seem to actually take pride in defying our need for sleep. I've heard people say, "I'll sleep when I'm dead!" Yeah, and you'll be dead sooner rather than later! This type of thinking is incredibly arrogant. Even Jesus grew weary and took time for rest. He slept on a boat (Mark 4:38). He sat down to rest when he was tired from his travels (John 4:6). When the demands of ministry became overwhelming, he said to his disciples, "Let's go off by ourselves to a quiet place and rest awhile" (Mark 6:31 NLT). If Jesus needed the fuel of rest to sustain his ministry, how much more do we need to rely on rest to fuel us for the fights of this life?

Proper rest is especially important when you're in a

difficult season—a marital problem, a job loss, crushing stress at work, a health crisis, parenting challenges, and more. When we are chronically fatigued, we are more likely to make poor decisions, to be irritable, and to get into accidents. In a marriage, that means a greater increase in the likelihood of quarreling.

Maybe you've heard the age-old cliche, "Don't go to bed angry." That specific quote is not in the Bible, though a variation of it exists, which says, "Do not let the sun go down while you are still angry" (Ephesians 4:26). Sometimes the best thing you can do *is* go to bed angry, pray about it, cool off, and revisit the issue refreshed the next day. The point of not going to bed angry isn't about fighting as long as it takes until someone wins or staying up until both of your hearts are clean and right; it's about keeping short accounts and not allowing small issues to fester into something larger.

When we're tired, we don't have the fuel we need to live and love well. When we're tired, we make regrettable decisions and say hurtful things. When we're tired, we are more vulnerable to doing a host of things we wouldn't normally do. For example, studies have shown that individuals who do not get adequate sleep are more likely to be involved in motor vehicle collisions.[4] Lack of sleep or poor sleep habits have also been shown to increase the risk of suicide by 34 percent.[5] Given all this, it's not hard to see how much more likely we are to make bad decisions in the heat of a marital conflict when we're tired.

Just as Jesus was tested and tempted by Satan, we, too,

will be tested and tempted. And the Enemy is more likely to attack not when we are at our strongest but when we are at our weakest. So why would we want to give our adversary an advantage when we don't have to? Find your battle rhythm for the fight by prioritizing rest. This isn't hard, but it does require intentionality. For example, you can increase the odds of getting a good night's sleep by beginning to rest even before you get into bed. Start by turning off your devices—smartphones, laptops, electronic games, and so on—at least an hour before going to bed. Try to go to bed and wake up at the same time each day. Avoid caffeinated beverages for six hours prior to bedtime. Consult with your doctor, a nutritionist, or other professionals to address issues that keep you from achieving optimal rest, especially if you are in a stressful season of life.

Jesus was fully equipped and completely prepared for the tests he faced in his earthly life because he was fueled for victory physically as well as spiritually. He was empowered by his unbroken fellowship with the Father. You have access to this same source of power as you fight for your marriage, your family, and your own health and well-being.

We Are Fueled for Victory When We Lead Like Jesus

One of the greatest lessons we can learn from Jesus to help us fight for our marriages is commitment. Commitment is what keeps us fighting for what matters most when things get really hard and we want to quit. As couples, we must be not only committed to each other but also mutually committed to Christ if we want to have healthy and steady marriages.

Being mutually committed to Christ means keeping our hearts tender and responsive to his teaching and leadership in our lives. There is no room for hardened hearts because of offenses or for power struggles or grudges. If every married couple made this commitment—to be intentional in their daily efforts to love selflessly—divorce rates, suicides, and substance abuse would no doubt be drastically reduced. Not to mention an increase in the number of marriages that are healthier and thriving! If we approached marriage with two hearts surrendered to Christ and submitted to each other out of reverence for Christ, we could overcome any challenges in our lives.

No marriage is free of conflict. Remember, Jesus promised we would have trouble in this life, and you can bet your marriage is included in that promise. But trouble is no excuse to quit when things get hard. Jesus did not say, "Go ahead and get married, and if things don't go as planned, you can divorce and get another spouse." In fact, he said quite the opposite.

Jesus said, "It has been said, 'Anyone who divorces his wife must give her a certificate of divorce.' But I tell you that anyone who divorces his wife, except for sexual immorality, makes her the victim of adultery, and anyone who marries a divorced woman commits adultery" (Matthew 5:31–32). According to Jesus, marriage is a lifelong commitment, and divorce as an escape clause for anything other than adultery is not an option.

This poses a challenge for every married couple. When the fiery darts of the Enemy are launched at you, your spouse, or your family, how will you respond? Will you draw on the fuel of your commitment, God's Word, and prayer, or will you look for the nearest escape route? This is a call from the mountaintops for every man and woman reading this book to take up the challenge to embrace marriage as Jesus exemplified through his Word. It begins in our hearts. That's the source of fuel, that's the power we need, that's what the battles of heaven and hell are contending for daily.

Victory in Jesus

There's a hymn called "Victory in Jesus" that many of us sang in church in years past and some may still sing today. Eugene Bartlett wrote and composed it in 1939, just two years before he died. One verse goes like this:

> And then I cried, "Dear Jesus, come and heal
> my broken spirit,"
> And somehow Jesus came and brought to me
> the victory.[6]

There's no victory without Jesus—not in our marriages, finances, careers, parenting, health, or any other area of our lives. Nothing of value in life can be attained without first submitting ourselves to the leadership and redemption we find in Jesus. He lifts the broken spirit, he cleanses wretched souls, and he heals the lives of men and women. We must commit to loving like him, living like him, resting like him, and leading like him. When we do, we experience victory through him! We won't always get it right, especially when our hearts become hardened because of the pain and trouble of this world. But we can always cry out, "Dear Jesus, come and heal my broken spirit!" And my friend, I promise you, somehow, Jesus will come and bring you the victory. That's the fuel we need. It can be found in our sweet surrender to the Good Shepherd, who hears our cries and awaits with open arms.

DISCUSSION

- Which of the four sources of fuel—loving like Jesus, living like Jesus, resting like Jesus, leading like Jesus—do you feel you need most in your marriage right now? Share the reasons for your response.
- We need proper rest to fuel us for the battles in this life. What practical changes can you make to be more intentional about consistently getting adequate sleep?
- Being mutually committed to Christ as husband and wife means keeping your hearts tender and responsive to his teaching and leadership in your lives.

What, if anything, has hardened your heart toward each other or made you less responsive to Christ? How do you think your relationship might change if your hearts were tender toward Jesus? Discuss any changes you plan to make to be more responsive to Jesus' teaching and leadership in your lives.

AFFIRMATION

We choose to surrender to Christ, and we do so together, daily. You are worthy of my selfless love. I commit to loving you as Jesus loves us. We are both recipients of his love and grace, and we will live as he taught us to live. We will be intentional about fueling our relationship in the way Jesus modeled for us. We can love like Jesus, live like Jesus, rest like Jesus, and lead like Jesus. In all these ways and more, we will live out our commitment to Christ and to each other, so we can be victorious in fighting for what matters most.

ACTION

The decisions and actions of yesterday are over. This is a new day, with new fuel for the fight and hearts surrendered to the Creator. It will require your complete surrender to Jesus to remain a vessel full of heaven's fuel for the fight. Write a few ways you can experience victory over the challenges of life together and how you can best prepare for conflict in this area.

CHAPTER 8

ACCESSING THE POWER

WHEN I HEAR PEOPLE OUTSIDE THE SPECIAL operations community talk about those who serve on special ops teams, they seem to think that these amazing warriors are nearly invincible, that they can take on any challenge and defeat the enemy all on their own. But even the highest levels of elite training and the most advanced tactical gear and equipment aren't enough to make these warriors indestructible. In fact, what makes them so effective at what they do is how heavily they rely on outside support to accomplish the mission and stay alive. Every aspect of support matters, whether it comes in the form of good intelligence, organized logistics, operational infrastructure, or hundreds of other intricate details that go into a successful mission. All that support gives the individual operators confidence, which is crucially important.

You need confidence when jumping out of an aircraft at 30,000 feet in the middle of the night while wearing 150 pounds of gear, and that only happens when you trust that the parachute rigger back on the ground has maintained your equipment and the pilot has accurately located the planned landing zone. Anyone who's had to operate in high-stakes conditions like these gets a resounding lesson that life's most challenging missions cannot be successfully completed alone. We all need support!

In life, we can do some things in our own power, but if we want to become the people and the spouses God created us to be, we need access to the life-changing power of the Holy Spirit. The Holy Spirit is the only power that enables us to live far above the limits of our own potential and capabilities. That's important because, just like special operations forces on the battlefield, you may find yourself well beyond the forward edge of the battle area (FEBA). In other words, deep in the Enemy territory.

As a marine I've heard many air force jokes, and I admit to telling a few myself. But the truth is, if you're a marine out on your own behind enemy lines and get caught by an enemy force of superior numbers and firepower, you need support—specifically, something called close air support (CAS). When you look up and see an A-10 Warthog operated by a US Air Force pilot on the horizon, well, it's the most beautiful sight in the world. You'll never forget it, not to mention the growling *brrrrrt* sound of the thirty-millimeter cannon raining down, wreaking havoc on the enemy. At that moment, even the most arrogant war fighters—and I've known a few—become believers that we cannot win battles alone. And those air force jokes are a distant memory.

That principle applies to the battlefields of life as much as it does the battlefields of combat. We were never meant to do life alone. God designed us for community, for fellowship, for us to support one another. The only caution is to identify your proper support system so you won't fall into the Enemy's trap that looks like support but isn't.

Identify Proper Support

When you step out onto the battlefields of life and wander into Enemy territory, which I define as the world we live in, you'd better have your CAS ready to go. Maybe you have never or will never serve in any capacity in the military. But we're all enlisted in a mission for the kingdom of God, deployed from heaven as ambassadors for the King, on a mission to tell the world about his redeeming love. In that role, you *are* in hostile territory, which means you'd better have backup standing by before you find yourself pinned down by the Enemy and realize you are overwhelmed and losing. You need to know whom to call on—and whom not to call on—for support.

As a married couple, when either of you experiences a crisis in life, your first line of support is each other. Never deviate from that. When you are fighting for your marriage, a crisis can be an opportunity for you to grow closer to each other and in your walk with Christ. But it can also be an opportunity for the Enemy to present some hellish tactics to divide your marriage and destroy your lives.

God has used tumultuous times to teach Kathy and me about having a covenant marriage. A covenant marriage model is about the unity and oneness between a man, a woman, and God. We get this model from one of the most popular verses relating to marriage today, which says, "Therefore a man shall leave his father and mother and be joined to his wife, and they shall become one flesh" (Genesis 2:24 NKJV). Discovering that we were not two individuals striving for selfish gain but one flesh under God gave Kathy and me our greatest tool to defeat the Enemy: *unity!* In the midst of the battles of life, we needed to be a unified force working as one team with one purpose, under the authority of Jesus. That's the goal for every marriage, including yours. This is why the Enemy will use every tool he has to create division between you and your spouse.

I once heard a fable about Satan and his mission to create division. The story provides a vivid picture of his strategy and plan. Here is how I remember it:

The end of days had come for Satan. God gave him his last days to wreak havoc on the Earth, but soon he had to close up shop. So Satan had a garage sale to sell all the tools he had used for thousands of years to destroy mankind.

When a man walked through the items for sale, he noticed every item had a different price tag on it, including many of Satan's greatest weapons of destruction. The most expensive price tag was $100 million, twice as high as any other tool. But the tool was just a crudely shaped wooden triangle. Confused as to why such a basic-looking tool would be so costly, the man asked Satan.

Satan said that it had been his most effective tool for destroying churches, marriages, families, and legacies. "This is a wedge," Satan said, "and I can use it to divide things that God meant to be together. I've even used it to separate human beings from God."

Satan's primary goal is to separate us from one another, and ultimately, to separate us from God.

For the first fifteen years of our marriage, Satan had been successful at keeping Kathy and me on our separate paths. However, once his plan was exposed and we discovered the power of unity, we began to make some changes.

Understanding that God intended for Kathy and me to be one flesh changed the way we handled conflict going forward. The word *divorce* no longer had a place in our relationship vocabulary. We gained a new perspective when we realized that the fight was not *between* Kathy and me but *for* Kathy and me—and *against* our common Enemy.

This perspective changed the way we view conflict. We now see each disagreement—about money, how we parent our kids, sex, and major life decisions—as that wooden triangle Satan wants to place between us, and we stop and agree not to let Satan do that to us. We seek God and, if necessary, wise counsel from others, so we can face the issue together and in unity.

To initiate such unity in marriage you must remain in oneness with your spouse and with Christ. What does that look like? For starters, here are two things it does *not* look like. It doesn't look like sharing your marital problems with a work colleague who has become your confidant. And it doesn't look like complaining about your spouse to a "friend" of the opposite sex. When you are fighting for your marriage, remaining in oneness looks like protecting your marriage. Remember, in times of crisis, you are more vulnerable to the attacks of the Enemy.

Relinquish Control

Today Kathy and I have a phenomenal marriage, but it wasn't always this way. We used to fight against each other often. Kathy knew exactly what to say to send me off the deep end when I hurt her; she can be a fireplug! Our fights were gauged by who could cut the other the deepest; victory was determined by who could scream the loudest and say the most hurtful things. When I look back at our fights, I can't even recall what most of them were about. The root cause of each dispute typically went unresolved as we both sought to win at all costs.

I now realize that one of our core issues was that we made little time for each other. Our hearts and minds were so cluttered with the busyness of life that even the littlest annoyances erupted into major wars. We were both full of toxic emotions and easily triggered. I sometimes use the analogy of a bottle of water to describe our fragile condition. When a bottle is half full, you can shake it around and it will barely spill a drop. However, when a bottle is full, the slightest motion will cause the contents to spill. Kathy and I were both filled to the brim with selfishness, bitterness, frustration, and anger. It didn't take much for us to spill all over each other. We were not in unity, and our selfishness drove us both to be very controlling. When we fought to remain in control and to win, we lost out on the best God had for us. We didn't realize it then, but there are times when we have to relinquish control and simply walk by faith.

My coauthor, Adam Davis, often refers to this kind of faith as "flashlight" faith. It's the kind of faith that illuminates only the next step or two. When life takes Adam into dark places and he cannot control every situation or outcome, he walks by flashlight faith. And it's biblical. The psalmist wrote, "Your word is a lamp for my feet, a light on my path" (Psalm 119:105). God never promised to illuminate the entire path ahead of us; he gives us just enough light to take the next step on the path.

When we walk in faith, we love and serve with open hands, trusting the light of God's Word and the power of his presence to guide and direct us. Loving and serving with open hands in marriage is difficult, and so is walking dark paths. It's human nature to want to control our circumstances, but we can't fight for control and still hope to be in unity with God and our spouses.

Fighting for control leads only to frustration, disappointment, and unnecessary arguments in marriage. Realizing God is the one who controls the outcome frees us from that burdensome mindset and puts us back in our roles as children of the King, instead of two people fighting each other to be king. Relinquish control to the Holy Spirit who will guide you through stressful situations, give you courage to face fear, and provide peace under pressure. All you need to do is ask him! It's that simple.

Maybe you're thinking, *But* how *do I ask him, and* what *do I ask him for?* Good questions. Asking God for power to get through the battles of life together looks a lot like surrendering to him. And that's exactly what it is. When we serve with open hands, our palms are open to heaven, ready to receive whatever God gives. We live freely from a place of complete surrender in the knowledge that God is sovereign over all things. All we're required to do is live in obedience to him, follow the light he gives us, and trust him. Yes, it is easier said than done in most cases. But we can live by flashlight faith. We simply have to be willing to take one step at a time and not grow anxious about all the other steps to come, knowing we may sometimes stumble. It's not uncommon to stumble when we're navigating dark and unfamiliar places.

I thought reaching the other side of the darkest times

in my life meant I would be free from struggle and never again have physiological stressors or symptoms of anxiety, panic, and depression. However, on the backside of dealing with PTSD, I still had to learn to relinquish control to God. Yes, I still get frustrated (though not as often), and I still experience brief moments when I feel hopeless. But now I know who is in control. For example, when our son Hunter was on deployment in Afghanistan, I experienced panic attacks, high blood pressure, a sense of hopelessness, and overwhelming fear. Then I opened my hands, released the reins, and relinquished control to God. And he gave me peace, he comforted me, and he restored my joy.

The trials of life don't go away; they only change forms and shapes. The difference between my initial battles with PTSD and now is how I handle it. Today I do my best to respond biblically. Instead of spiraling out of control and suffering in silence, I pray, study the Bible, talk to Kathy, and seek support from my closest brothers. It sounds really basic, but that's actually a good thing. In the midst of battle, our minds tend to become cloudy and confused. Having a simple strategy in place makes it easier to implement when the rounds start firing a little too close to home.

How to Recognize God's Support System

We've talked previously about having a mentor couple, but each spouse should also have a godly mentor or a good friend to confide in one-on-one. Men need mentors who are godly men; women need mentors who are godly women. Godly mentors are those who are seasoned, wise, biblically literate, strong in faith, compassionate, and willing to walk with you through your trials. In his book *Disciplines of a Godly Man*, R. Kent Hughes wrote:

> Men, if you're married, your wife must be your most *intimate* friend, but to say "My wife is my best friend" can be a cop-out. You also need Christian male friends who have a same-sex understanding of the serpentine passages of your heart, who will not only offer counsel and pray for you but will also hold you accountable to your commitments and responsibilities when necessary.[1]

And the same principle holds true for women. We all need someone who understands the challenges we face from the inside out.

Another key characteristic to look for in a mentor is that they are more concerned about your marriage than they are about your personal comfort, opinions, or success. If your friends aren't friends of your marriage, they aren't the friends you need in your life. Both of you need mentoring relationships with godly individuals of the same sex who can walk with you through life.

Here's one caution: be careful who you confide in, especially when you're in crisis. Some may be more interested in wallowing with you in pain than they are in seeing you get through the struggle in a godly fashion. Maybe you've heard the phrase "misery loves company." In the sixteenth century, a play was written about a man named Doctor Faustus who agreed to sell his soul to the devil in exchange for twenty-four years of life with his desires being fulfilled.[2] When asked why Satan sought to enlarge his kingdom, Mephistopheles, the devil's agent who brokered the deal with Faustus, essentially replied, "Misery loves company." In other words, Satan can use others to keep us stuck in our misery and separated from God and our spouses.

The Enemy seeks to kill, steal, and destroy (John 10:10), and he can use others to execute his divisive strategy in our lives. Avoid confidants who would rather drag you into a pit of misery than help you get to the other side. And when you are the confidant, the mentor, the friend, be the person who seeks to guide others with the promises of God's Word, someone who is transparent, honest, and Christlike.

When you're in the midst of a crisis, a godly confidant will support you with biblical principles and a heart of compassion. But they will also shoot straight with you by speaking the truth and not sugarcoat the reality of your situation. God gave us companionship, relationship, and community to support us. When we rely on our own strength and power to overcome, we position ourselves for defeat. We must take God at his word. Obey him, follow the path he has laid before us, do the work he has called us to do, and trust him with the rest.

If you want to see God's support system, look around

you. It's near you. It's likely in the same room with you or otherwise close to you in some way. Nobody is coming to save you. So, when you feel hopeless, where do you turn? Your first line of defense is God, and your second line of defense is your spouse. Cling to each other in the heat of battle. Notice when your spouse may need a little more kindness and compassion when you're both going through the hard places. You must be resilient as a couple through the trials of life, or the Enemy will use them to divide and conquer you. That's always been his strategy.

When we remain in fellowship with God through prayer, studying his Word, and surrounding ourselves with godly people, we live in the presence of his truth and have access to God's resources—that includes the power of the Holy Spirit and the CAS of our spouse and mentors. When we're cut off from our support systems, we are vulnerable to the attacks of Satan. In battle, the enemy strategically lures us into isolation. We're easier to kill that way. Be hard to kill by remaining as one with your spouse and in fellowship with like-minded brothers and sisters, your family, and the church. This is the CAS you need in order to keep fighting for what matters most.

Requesting Assistance Requires Humility

The world will tell you to find yourself and rely on yourself, but God's Word tells you to give your life to God so that he may show you the way. Author and pastor Max Lucado said it best in his book *Experiencing the Heart of Jesus*:

The wizard [of Oz] says look inside yourself and find self.
God says look inside yourself and find God.
　　The first will get you to Kansas.
　　The latter will get you to heaven.
　　Take your pick.[3]

The role of the Holy Spirit is to be our comforter, helper, and teacher. There's no yellow brick road, but there are plenty of hazards along the way. Often *we* are the one (and the only) hazard we can control. No, looking inside yourself and finding yourself won't get you to some magical fairy tale fantasy land; it'll leave you empty as a used-up magazine. Though most of us understand that God and others are available to help us, it seems the only time we are prompted to ask for assistance is when we feel empty or are in pain. In his book *Whisper: How to Hear the Voice of God*, author and pastor Mark Batterson wrote, "You can leave the Bible on your bedside table untouched. You can ignore desires, dreams, doors, promptings, and people. But you can't ignore pain, can you?"[4]

Pain is a powerful motivator. When we experience pain, we are prompted to move. But moving must be done in the right way and in the right direction. We cannot ignore pain for too long, or it will debilitate us. The key is to keep our spiritual immune system strong, our faith muscles ready, and our skills with the weapons of spiritual warfare in tune before the pain presents itself. This is why we are more prone to pray when crisis is present than when things are going well. This is why we tend to pray more when someone is diagnosed with a terminal illness as opposed to when they are healthy. A lack of spiritual discipline causes us to get into a place of overwhelming pain; a certain degree of pride causes us to think we can handle it on our own; or maybe we lean into a degree of ignorance, thinking if we ignore the pain, it will just disappear.

Pain will cause you to feel hopeless and powerless. But when we look to God and rely on the Holy Spirit, hell's strategy for pain in our lives is flipped. When you are in crisis, you can move toward a temporary, unreliable, and unproven solution, or you can move toward God. His Word promises that when we draw near to him, he will draw near to us (James 4:8). In his presence, we will discover purpose, true power, the peace we desperately sought in other sources, and finally, the great comfort and healing we needed all along. He is the support we need to guide us through times of prosperity and times of crisis.

Build on the Rock

Jesus once told a story about the importance of building a house on the right foundation. He said:

Therefore everyone who hears these words of mine and puts them into practice is like a wise man who built his house on the rock. The rain came down, the streams rose, and the winds blew and beat against that house; yet it did not fall, because it had its foundation on the rock. But everyone who hears these words of mine and does not put them into practice is like a foolish man who built his house on sand. The rain came down, the streams rose, and the winds blew and beat against that house, and it fell with a great crash. (Matthew 7:24–27)

On what foundation have you built your marriage? If it's anything other than Christ, it's a foundation built on sand, which will crumble in a storm.

I've heard a lot of people say, "Give me a simple path to fix my life; show me how to fix my marriage." When I send them to Jesus, some tend to scowl. Listen, I am unashamedly pointing you to Christ. There's no five-step plan to fix all the problems you may be facing; there's only one step. Once you find Jesus, he will guide you through the path you need to take. That's the beautiful thing about the love of Jesus. He doesn't ask us to clean ourselves up before we come to him. Instead, he welcomes us as we are, and his love restores and revitalizes our lives.

If you want to access the only power that can truly change your life and your marriage, Jesus is the way. Your part is to collaborate with him by practicing spiritual disciplines that will strengthen your foundation from the inside out. That's part of what it means to hear the words of Jesus and put them into practice. Author and pastor Dallas Willard described spiritual disciplines as "activities we engage in that are within our power and enable us to do what we cannot do by direct effort."[5] In other words, spiritual disciplines are strength-training exercises that empower us over time to live the life God calls us to and become the people he created us to be.

There are many spiritual disciplines, but some foundational ones include prayer and spending time with God in solitude and silence, studying the Bible, worshipping, sharing life in community with like-minded believers, observing a Sabbath rest, stewarding gifts and resources, and engaging in acts of service for love of Christ. The goal is not necessarily to practice all the disciplines at once but to choose the ones that best suit your needs now and practice them consistently. Pray daily, study the Bible together regularly, commit to a small group, and practice consistent and generous giving. Just as regular workouts at the gym build muscle strength and stamina over time, consistent practice of spiritual disciplines builds spiritual strength and stamina over time. When the storms of life come, your foundation will be strong and anchored to the rock of Christ.

Requesting assistance is not a sign of weakness. In fact, one of the things I pray daily is for God to give me the strength, wisdom, and willpower to address whatever challenges come my way. Yes, this requires consistency in your walk with Christ, not from a legalistic standpoint but from one of discipline rooted in love for him. If you need help, ask for it. Humility is a powerful tool for those who want to live victorious lives.

DISCUSSION

- How would you describe the current CAS available to you, both as individuals and as a couple? What support systems do you have in place?
- In what ways, if any, might God be inviting you to relinquish control in your marriage and to walk by flashlight faith?
- In what ways has the devil used his favorite tool to come between you and your spouse? Consider past as well as recent examples. Also reflect on how his strategy changes or remains the same during times of crisis or stress.
- What spiritual disciplines might you begin to practice as a couple? Set realistic and achievable goals to create momentum for practicing these disciplines.

AFFIRMATION

God is my primary support system, but I am thankful he has also given us each other to navigate through this life together. Because of the Holy Spirit, we have the power to live a victorious life and have a thriving marriage. I promise to honor you and cling to you in crisis, to devote my life to becoming more Christlike, and to be present for you in times of peace and in times of tribulation. Until death do us part, I give you my heart, and, together, we present our lives to God.

ACTION

- Wherever you find yourself at this moment, create a plan now for CAS—with God, each other, and mentors/friends. Identify two or three steps you will take over the next week to implement your plan.
- Choose one or two spiritual disciplines and make a plan to practice them consistently together for twenty-one days. Secure any resources you might need and block out time on your calendar. At the end of twenty-one days, reflect on what you've learned and make any necessary adjustments. Then keep practicing.

ROUND V

PUT YOURSELF SECOND

CHAPTER 9

JESUS FIRST ... ALWAYS

PUTTING YOUR PERSONAL STORY OUT THERE IS hard. It's never comfortable or convenient. And if you're authentic and honest, you may feel insecure, embarrassed, or ashamed. Yet it is necessary. It's an essential step in your healing, it's essential for the healing of others, and it's all part of God's plan.

If you've ever struggled with depression, anxiety, or shame over sin, chances are that a counselor or mentor has encouraged you to "get it off your chest," "let it out," or "unload." But when you're dealing with hard things, "talking about it" isn't usually at the top of your list, especially if shame is involved. You believe the lie that no one would understand what you're up against or what it's like to be you in the middle of the mess. As a result, you feel backed into a corner, alone and without hope. But this is *not true*.

In *Tender Warrior*, pastor Stu Weber wrote, "So

everything that's killing you is somewhere in the chest of every man you know."[1] In other words, the struggles you think are unique to you are actually common to all of us. The challenge is having the courage to speak it, to step out of your comfort zone and share your struggles with others. In fact, God not only wants you to but also calls you to do so, because it is part of his plan to save the world.

There is a fascinating account of this in the book of Revelation, which describes a great war in heaven between God's angels and a dragon, the "ancient serpent called the devil, or Satan, who leads the whole world astray" (12:9). When the dragon and his fallen angels lost the fight and were hurled to earth, a "loud voice in heaven" (v. 10) proclaimed God's victory, saying:

> They triumphed over him
>> by the blood of the Lamb
>> and by the word of their testimony. (v. 11)

The "they" at the start of the sentence is not the angels but us, human beings. And what was the key to our victory over Satan? Our salvation purchased by the blood of the Lamb—our testimony, our stories of how God saved us.

That's how powerful your story is, and why your story is part of God's plan to save the world. Someone out there is hurting and struggling to find hope, and they need to hear your story. Share it. Whether you stand before an audience of millions or an audience of one, share it. Share where you were, where you are now, and where you are headed. If Christ has given you a victory in your life, share it with the enthusiasm of someone who was rescued from death—because you were. If you are still struggling, share that too. Others need to know they are not alone. Share your powerful story and be part of God's master plan for changing the world.

Keep in mind that the Enemy is fully aware of God's strategy and will do anything to keep you from telling your story. He will tell you you're not good enough. He will make accusations against you, heaping you with shame, guilt, and anxiety to silence you. Stand against Satan's tactics and fight. The world is at stake; others' lives and eternities are at stake. It won't be easy, but what battle worth fighting is easy? The worthiest victories always come on the other side of the most challenging battles. So, no, it won't be easy, but it will be worth it.

I Am Second

When Kathy and I first started the Mighty Oaks Foundation, I had a deep desire to help other veterans and their families, but I had no interest in public speaking. Which is why I felt uncomfortable and almost said no when my good friend Dave Roever asked me to speak at a small church in Michigan on Veterans Day. But Dave is one of those people I respect too much to say no to, so I went. As it turned out, this "small church" was attended by nearly twenty thousand people, and it was my first experience of publicly sharing my story.

I was so insecure that I couldn't imagine even one person caring about what I had to say. But I felt called to do it, and I had a sense of peace about sharing the story of what God had done in my life. To my surprise, hundreds of people lined up to talk to me afterward, some just to shake my hand and others to share how their story connected with mine. One woman told me she had lost her son to a drunk driver and my words helped her reconcile her loss. Another man who was separated from his wife and children and was planning to divorce said my words convicted him, and now he was taking his family to lunch after the service. These encounters deeply affected me. I understood that God could use the story of what Christ had done in my life to help others, to let them know that they were not alone and that Jesus could help them too.

I felt motivated to speak, write, and share my story, and I began to do so more and more. I've been blessed to speak at some prominent venues, like Liberty University in front of an audience of fifteen thousand, as well as many incredible churches and military commands. But during those early years, there weren't many events as large as that first church in Michigan. A breakout moment presented itself when my friend and former US Navy SEAL soldier Remi Adeleke contacted me. Remi was with I Am Second, a not-for-profit organization created to inspire people to put Jesus first.

I Am Second started in 2008 by telling twenty stories of

real people through short films. As their website describes, "The real people in these stories came from a mix of backgrounds but their theme rang consistent. Like so many people, they had tried living for themselves, but it left them addicted, alone, purposeless, and lost. Only when they put Jesus first in their lives did they find peace and freedom."[2] I Am Second has told stories through more than 140 films, featuring actors, athletes, musicians, business leaders, addicts, survivors, and next-door neighbors. And because of their bravery, I Am Second's content has been viewed more than 150 million times in over 230 countries/territories.

When Remi asked if I'd be willing to share my story, I didn't really know the reach of the platform. But I knew it was an excellent opportunity to reach people, and so I decided to go for it. The other thing I didn't know was how intense the interview process would be. I Am Second typically interviews skilled communicators who are well practiced at sharing their stories, so their process intentionally tries to get beyond those polished exteriors and peel back layer after layer to bring out the raw emotions of the speaker.

The process started with written questions over email. Many of the questions were about the same issues but asked in different ways. I answered them three times through email before moving on to a phone interview. Then came filming day. I sat on a white leather chair in a pitch-black room. Even the camera people wore black, so I couldn't see them. Above me were blinding white lights. Behind me, out of sight, was the interviewer, although it felt like he was more of an interrogator. He asked the same questions over and over in different ways, peeling back the layers and going deeper. At the time of the interview, I had been sharing my story for a few years and had probably done so over a hundred times, but I had never experienced so many emotions all at the same time while doing it—stirred, agitated, regretful, joyful, and passionate. The I Am Second team achieved their goal of drawing out my emotions.

Although the finished video is only fourteen minutes, the filming took over three hours. A few weeks later, when I saw the first cut, I couldn't make it through the whole thing because it was too raw. When I finally did make it through to the end, I wanted to crawl under the table. I was so uncomfortable seeing myself that exposed. It took everything in me to share the video with a few very close friends to see what they thought. They loved it, which was actually not the reaction I wanted. I was hoping they would tell me it wouldn't make the cut and would never be published. When I expressed my concerns to Luis, a retired Navy SEAL and one of my teammates at Mighty Oaks, and told him how I wanted to pull the plug on the whole project, he responded, "That's why it's so important you share it." I'm so thankful for men like Luis in my life, who will tell me what I need to hear when I need to hear it. So I went ahead with the video.

Today more than one million people have seen it. I have received hundreds, if not thousands, of messages from people about how the video has affected them and led them to a decision point of change, many leading to a relationship with Christ. What a blessing and an honor. I still have a hard time watching the video, especially in front of others, but what makes my discomfort worth it is the gratitude I feel to God for using my story to rescue others.

God is first; I Am Second.

Putting God first is the foundational principle for a godly life and a godly marriage. When we learn to apply this principle of surrendering to God daily, we become better spouses, and our marriages are better positioned to overcome the challenges of life.

True Leadership Is Selfless

Through my years of being deployed in Afghanistan, the traditional roles in our family became blurred. Kathy had to take on all the roles to keep the family together and moving forward. She never called me in Afghanistan to tell me the washing machine wasn't working or to complain that she had to somehow get three kids to ten destinations in one day, because she knew I couldn't do anything about it. I think she always viewed her role as a warrior's wife who could hold things together. It was comforting for me to know that our home and children were in good hands, but it was a pretty big load for Kathy to carry by herself. She is an amazing mom, but she also had to fill in as "dad." She is an amazing wife, but she also had to fill in as "husband."

She did it all and didn't complain, because she knew I

needed that kind of support to do my job. And it worked for us for a season. However, when I came home for good, we struggled to redefine our marriage roles, which previously had Kathy caring for our children and home while I served what seemed to be one deployment after another. And even when I was home, I wasn't fully present because I was struggling with my PTSD. We understood what our marriage roles should be as the Bible defined them, but that didn't make them any easier to live out, especially when we had both become accustomed to living life differently.

Military wives rise to the occasion, taking the reins when their husbands are deployed, and then give the reins back when their husbands come home. But often men are unable to maintain that leadership role consistently and only play the part when it's convenient for them to do so. When husbands don't show up consistently in all areas of their biblical responsibility to lead, wives tend to fill the void. Then, sooner or later, a power struggle ensues, which can turn into chaos in the home.

Often, when I challenge men to take charge in their homes, they tell me it won't work in their marriages. A man who does not lead his family will prompt his wife to fill the void, and this displacement of roles will lead to conflict between the husband and wife. So what does it mean to lead? Does it mean men are domineering, somehow superior, or in charge? The Bible clearly states that men and women are equal, but it also says that husbands and wives have different roles. These biblical roles are one of the most controversial and misused interpretations of marriage. If there is confusion or conflict about these roles in your marriage, you will always work against the grain. In fact, I would say that following the biblical roles for marriage is second only to being unified with God as the foundational key to success.

The apostle Paul described the nature of the relationship between husband and wife when he wrote:

> For the husband is the head of the wife as Christ is the head of the church, his body, of which he is the Savior. Now as the church submits to Christ, so also wives should submit to their husbands in everything.
>
> Husbands, love your wives, just as Christ loved the church and gave himself up for her. (Ephesians 5:23–25)

Some men have a tendency to focus on just two phrases: "the husband is the head" and "wives should submit." But we need to take the passage as a whole for deeper understanding.

The model for the husband's role is Jesus Christ and his relationship to the church. Jesus' example is that of sacrificial love and service. There is not a more perfect example of servant leadership than that! Was Jesus head of the church? Yes. But he also gave himself up for her.

As husbands, we have to ask ourselves, "To what lengths am I willing to go to be a servant leader in my marriage?" I sometimes hear men joke, "I'd die for my wife, but I draw the line at taking out the trash!" Jesus showed us that there are no limits to servanthood; he gave his life for us. Speaking of himself, Jesus said, "For even the Son of Man did not come to be served, but to serve, and to give his life as a ransom for many" (Mark 10:45). *Jesus came to serve.* We miss the mark when we expect our spouses to serve us. When Scripture says the "husband is the head" in the marriage, don't take it out of context. If you want to lead your wife and be the head of your family, it means you are the chief servant in the relationship. That's what it takes to love your wife as Christ loved the church.

I get the opportunity to teach this principle to military men through our ministry. Ironically, even with a military divorce rate at over 80 percent for combat veterans, this servant leadership model makes sense to them. I sometimes explain it like this: Imagine you're in an infantry platoon in Afghanistan, and as you're establishing an objective rally point to conduct your mission, the officer in charge issues some orders and then kicks his feet up while everyone else is digging defensive positions. Would you follow this guy? No. We all follow the leader who stands with us shoulder to shoulder, busting rocks and pulling his weight, getting dirty and leading by example. That's the kind of leader troops will follow and for whom they would die.

Now, everyone who knows a little about military chains of command knows that the officer in charge will always have a "number two" leader. The crazy thing about the number twos in the military is that they are typically the most experienced. That new lieutenant fresh out of college and Officer Candidate School may be motivated to lead with all his academic knowledge, but the number two in his command is a crusty old staff sergeant who has ten times the street smarts. Many young lieutenants gain their best leadership insights from the first platoon sergeant who reported to them. The military does a brilliant job of creating a balance of positional authority and experiential wisdom, bringing both together to form a unit capable of success and growth.

We see this similar model in marriage. The husband is in the position of authority and the wife is in the position of number two; she is the source of knowledge, intuition, and wisdom. Both are perfectly equal, occupying different but equally meaningful roles. Marriage is a perfect and beautiful unit designed for success and growth.

The process starts with a husband taking on his role as a servant leader, humbling himself, and accepting responsibility for everyone under his authority, including himself. I have seen families restored when husbands took the lead in filling their biblical role in a marriage covenant. I have witnessed wives who found joy and relief when they no longer had to carry the burden they were never meant to carry. I have seen children grow in their faith as biblical roles of godly leadership were modeled in their homes. Leadership is responsibility.

When a man of God humbles himself, takes responsibility, and fully submits to God's leadership, the Lord restores his family, and his wife and children trust and follow his leadership. Servant leadership is based on the principle that others come before you, your spouse comes before you, and nobody comes before God in your life. This is a beautiful image of how our marriages should be—with God on the throne of our hearts!

The Pedestal Principle

The pedestal principle is an image of marriage that consists of three parts. The first leg of the pedestal represents the husband, an imperfect man stained with sin but clothed with mercy and sustained by grace. The second leg represents the wife, a woman who has surrendered to her Lord, loves her husband, and seeks to honor God above all else. But these two legs alone can't fully support the pedestal; they need a third. The third leg represents the presence of the Holy Spirit. His presence is what stabilizes and strengthens marriages.

The seat on top of the three legs is reserved for God, who must be Lord of our marriages in order for us to overcome the challenges we face. Each leg is necessary, and the pedestal only stands strong when all three legs function together, and we glorify God above ourselves.

One of the challenges in marriage comes when we, husbands and wives, end up fighting for what we think is our spot on the seat of that pedestal. However, the only one with a rightful claim to that seat is Jesus. Now and always. When we fight to lift him high, when we fight to place his principles and his ways above our own, the pedestal of our marriage is strong and stable.

The character of God is a pure and selfless love that is truly unconditional. And when we read Scripture that says, "Husbands, love your wives, just as Christ loved the church," it can be confusing. A lot of men are willing to die for their wives, just like a lot of Christians say they are willing to die for their faith. But I don't think it's really about our willingness to die physically as much as it is about our willingness to die to self and live selflessly. When we invite Jesus into our hearts to become our Lord and Savior, it means we die to our own ways and surrender to his way.

Many have heard a popular teaching about "dying daily." Jesus said, "Whoever wants to be my disciple must deny themselves and take up their cross daily and follow me" (Luke 9:23). So when the apostle Paul mentioned dying to the flesh, he wasn't only referring to the hazards and threats he encountered in his travels as a missionary. When we make a decision to follow Jesus and take up our crosses, we make a decision to die to our old desires that do not align with his Word. Dying daily means, more specifically, putting God before ourselves and loving others selflessly. By God's grace and through Jesus we are a new creation (Colossians 3:10), ever growing, ever learning, and ever experiencing a renewed mind through the study of God's Word (Romans 12:2). We serve best when we serve with hearts full of Jesus and do not surrender to our flesh or to the power of sin.

True fulfillment in marriage comes when we place a higher priority on honoring God, abiding in his Word, and serving our spouses than we do on getting our own way.

That's it. Any other pursuits leave us empty. And when husbands try to "lead" using an authoritarian or dictatorial approach, it fractures the beauty of intimacy God intended for married couples to experience. Serve God; and the best place to start doing that is by serving your spouse in love.

Second to None

Marriage is more than men taking out the trash or women respecting their husbands. Remember earlier when I told you about the men who said, "I'd die for my wife, but I draw the line at taking out the trash"? That small gesture of taking out the trash, well, it shows those men are present. It shows how those men understand the big picture, which is about expressing love in service. It shows the world real men still exist. Healthy masculinity leads to healthy marriages, and godly men are servant leaders when they love like Christ. I know Kathy loves it when I lead our family as a man surrendered to Christ, and when I love her selflessly.

Be obedient to God's Word; don't just chase what makes you happy. It's not always about "what's in it for me." No, we serve to serve. Period. We honor our wives, and our wives honor us, because it is the right thing to do, not because there's a carrot dangling at the end of a stick.

Christ is second to no one. If we call him Lord, he must be Lord of everything in our lives, including our marriages, our femininity, and our masculinity. He must be Lord of it all. When we make his lordship our priority, the rest of the goodness life has to offer is icing on the cake. After Christ, your spouse is a close second. Aside from the King of kings, nobody, and I mean nobody, comes before your spouse. Fight for that. Fight to serve. Fight to prioritize your marriage. When you do, there's going to be less fighting between you and your spouse.

The way we love, the way we lead, and the way we address conflict is based a great deal on our stories. Our stories, such as the one I shared with I Am Second, are incredibly powerful.

If your stories aren't as glamorous as others', it's okay. Learn from them. If you were selfish in the past and it led you to experience conflict and adversity in your relationships, use those lessons to serve your spouse well. Use the stories of your life as fuel to be a better husband, a better wife, a better parent, but most of all, a better servant leader. When you do, you exemplify the life of Jesus, who gave his life for those he loved, including you.

DISCUSSION

- The stories of what God has done for us have spiritual power. Scripture states that our testimonies have the power to help us triumph over Satan (Revelation 12:11). How would you tell the story of your marriage right now? What is the testimony you want to share about your marriage?

- Jesus defined servant leadership when he said, "Whoever wants to become great among you must be your servant, and whoever wants to be first must be your slave—just as the Son of Man did not come to be served, but to serve, and to give his life as a ransom for many" (Matthew 20:26–28). For Christians, all leadership is servant leadership. In what ways do you want to practice this kind of leadership in your home?
- What marriage roles did you witness growing up? In what ways was that model positive or negative? How has it influenced your expectations for your own marriage?
- In what ways, if any, do you want your marriage roles to change?

AFFIRMATION

I am here. I choose to be present with you. You have my undivided attention in this moment. I promise to serve you with excellence, to honor you, and to honor God. You deserve the best from me. You come second to God alone. For the rest of our days together, I commit my life to serving you, loving you, and giving my life for you as a daily and living sacrifice to our Lord. He is Lord of my mind, my heart, and my body, and he is Lord of our marriage. He is second to none, and we are second to him.

ACTION

I talk to a lot of couples who go to bed with their smartphones in hand. As I travel the country, I see so many sad images of couples eating dinner with both of them looking at their phones. This is one way to evaluate what takes first place in your life, what comes before your relationship with God or your spouse. We've covered a lot of ground to this point, and you have been given a lot of tools. Note some things you can remove from your life to make room for these new tools, to make space for a better relationship with God and for a healthier marriage. For example, monitor your screen time. Eliminate the phone use in your bedroom and at the dinner table. Be present. That's the best way to put the person in front of you before yourself.

CHAPTER 10

STRENGTH FOR ALL SEASONS

WE HAD JUST REACHED THE ROUNDABOUT called Massoud Circle, a landmark dedicated to a national hero of Afghanistan, when the traffic jammed up and a Toyota Hilux stopped about fifteen yards in front of us, blocking our way forward. The truck was full of men armed with AK-47 assault rifles and even an RPG. They started to pile out the back of the Hilux, and I vividly remember locking eyes with the man who exited the front passenger door of the truck with his AK-47.

In training this is called being "stuck on the X"; the X being an ambush point or a kill zone. We were now on it. Among the skills I learned in training was to recognize when you are on the X, and then to get off it. Simple Marine Corps logic: you can't stay there or something bad is going to happen. I know if we had stayed on the X that day, we would have put up a heck of a fight, but we also would likely have been taken or killed.

One thing I love about the military is its training. For every scenario, we train over and over to the point of redundancy. So when the day for action comes, we don't have to decide what to do; we just do it. At the driving training school, we had been through this scenario a dozen times, and we were taught to solve a roadblock like the one in front of us with a ramming technique. So I floored the gas and aimed my vehicle directly at theirs.

One of my favorite memories from Afghanistan is when I crashed into that Hilux and saw Taliban guys flying out the back of it. It was a perfect hit, and their vehicle spun out of our way. But after smashing a clear path off the X, there was still another obstacle: what appeared to be a one-hundred-year-old policeman in his sharp blue uniform giving me an aggressive hand gesture to stop and frantically blowing his traffic whistle. I revved my engine and aimed the Toyota Prado I was driving toward him. The officer quickly switched allegiance to jump aboard the winning team and waved me out of harm's way, even stopping other cars for me to clear the scene.

To this day, I don't know what the intent was for that attack on us at Massoud Circle. I have my suspicions, but the truth is that if we had stopped on the X that day, I likely wouldn't be writing this book. What kept me moving forward was proper training and a belief that adhering to that training would lead to victory.

Having faith in something and believing that it will result in victory will always give you the ability to press forward in times when all seems hopeless—when you find yourself stuck on the X. Just imagine what life might be like if you could routinely have similar confidence and faith, the kind I had that day in Kabul that enabled me to overcome the obstacles I faced. Here's the good news: you can!

There is never a moment in your life when God is not available to you, and his plans for you are always good. Remember this promise? "'For I know the plans I have for you,' declares the LORD, 'plans to prosper you and not to harm you, plans to give you hope and a future'" (Jeremiah 29:11). God offers this promise to each of us, so when the day of adversity comes and we find ourselves on the X, we can be assured that moving forward will lead us to victory. It's not a promise that exempts us from the hardships of this world. But when we trust this promise and build strength with spiritual disciplines over time, we can be assured that on the other side of hardships, we will find ourselves where we are meant to be.

I wish I could say that I always reverted to my military training to get off the X in life, but there were many times I failed to press forward when I should have. In fact, only a few years after the incident at the roundabout, I was diagnosed with PTSD and came home feeling completely lost, ashamed, scared, and hopeless. I was on the X again, but this time I didn't follow the rules. I didn't recognize that I was on the X, and I didn't take the necessary steps to get off it. In life as well as in combat, choosing to stay on the X will almost certainly lead to our demise, literally or figuratively.

When Kathy and I recognized how this principle applied to our marriage, it changed everything. We realized that overcoming obstacles in our marriage meant we had to battle, and that meant we had to be a team and fight for each other. We got to that point by moving forward—applying the power of God's Word, utilizing the wisdom of my military training, and drawing on the support of friends and family. And we're here today, still choosing to move forward and fight for each other.

Creating a Safe Place to Heal

Each season of married life—from being newlyweds and new parents to empty nesters and beyond—presents unique challenges. The day Kathy and I were married, it never crossed our minds that trauma and life would have such an impact on our marriage. We vowed a commitment to stick it out "for better or for worse." But trauma? No way!

Our Mighty Oaks Foundation ministry is devoted to members of the service community and their families. By service community, we mean those who serve in the active duty and veterans of the US Armed Forces as well as those who served or are serving as first responders, including law enforcement officers, firefighters, EMTs, paramedics, and disaster relief workers. Most people don't consider how their service to our nation and communities will affect their minds, emotions, bodies, and spirits, much less their marriages. That was certainly the case for Kathy and me. No service member or first responder completes their service unscathed. Kathy and I fight not only for each other but also for these couples, because trauma almost beat us, and we want to help them beat the odds too. Knowing that suicide claims the lives of twenty military people every day, and that a failed relationship is a factor in 42 percent of them, we believe saving a marriage is literally life-saving work.

We know if we can get to the core—the marriage—we can have a positive impact on the rates of suicide and substance abuse. That's why we want to create a safe place for members of the service community to heal from the trauma and the evil they are exposed to. And marriage is supposed to be that safe place for healing, hope, love, and acceptance. Our purpose is to help service couples thrive, and so it is critical that we address how trauma affects a marriage.

One of the key characteristics of a resilient couple is a willingness to acknowledge the threats and challenges they face. It's impossible to experience healing while in a state of denial. So we must identify trauma, recognize its effects, and be willing to deal with it. Throughout this chapter, you will discover some of the key challenges faced by couples where trauma is present and how to find healing.

Not All Trauma Looks the Same, but All Trauma Needs Healing

When we discuss trauma within the service community, we are referring primarily to critical incidents.

Critical incidents are best defined as sudden and powerful events that are not part of your normal daily life. A few examples would be an officer-involved use of force, a combat situation for deployed military, or maybe a natural disaster or the sudden loss of a loved one. The same kind of incident may have a different impact on different people. For service members, trauma may be related to combat or other military-related events. For first responders, trauma is typically related to witnessing or helping others through tragedy. However, even when service community members have not experienced trauma at work, there are often traumatic experiences from childhood that had a profound impact on their lives. No one traumatic incident is the same, so it would be foolish to compare or rank experiences. All trauma leaves a legacy and needs to be taken seriously by a married couple.

Just as your pain won't look like my pain, your healing won't look like my healing. And there is no standard timeline for healing. No one can look at a trauma calendar and say, "Hey, I will be healed by this date." Your healing may take hours, months, years, or the rest of your life. Whether your trauma is the result of your service or some other event, your wounds are real, and your pain is real. Thankfully, healing is also real, especially if you will work together with your spouse and with God for that healing.

If you have not experienced trauma but your spouse has, let me help you here: you are never tasked with healing your spouse. Your role is to walk alongside and be supportive on their journey toward healing. You are to love your spouse, care for your spouse, and be present with your spouse. You are not responsible for fixing your spouse. But healing requires commitment—from both of you.

As a couple, you must be committed to creating a safe place where healing is welcome. Your marriage becomes a safe place when you offer support, validation, trust, respect, and acceptance. Without trying to be the fixer, you are free to be present for each other and to demonstrate a love that is real, powerful, and lasting.

Within the context of a safe place, one of the first things to do together on your journey toward healing is to acknowledge the pain and take it to God. There is no darkness that God's light cannot pierce. God is bigger than your trauma. God is not the author "of fear, but of power and of love and of a sound mind" (2 Timothy 1:7 NKJV). You can persevere together in the presence of pain and adversity because your love is worth the fight.

We cannot heal when we hide our trauma from God and others. Covering up a wound only makes it worse. It is up to you to work with God to heal what is broken. Jesus is the one who restores and heals; your responsibility is to give your trauma to him. What you have experienced will always be a part of your past, but its effects don't have to last forever. The scar may remain, but not the pain. Acknowledge the trauma you have faced, so you can receive the healing you need for yourself and your marriage. Don't diagnose or try to treat each other; instead, take responsibility to find the help you need when you need it. It is not your spouse's job to fix you; it is your spouse's job to love and support you.

The Price We Pay

"Thank you for your service," the gentleman said while my Marine Corps buddies and I waited for a table at a local restaurant. We never knew how to respond to such expressions of gratitude. I sometimes wonder how much people who haven't been in the military really understand about the toll our service takes on our families and marriages, and about all the sacrifices military families make from being away for such extended periods of time. Unless you've been through it yourself, it's hard to understand the experiences of those who serve at home and abroad, or how veterans react to certain triggers, how they isolate, and how they cope. Yet this is part of the decision when we choose to serve.

When considering life as the spouse of a military member or first responder, most of us don't think about the costs ahead of time. We simply fall in love and want to be with that person. And yet, counting the costs is essential in making any commitment. Jesus said, "For which of you, intending to build a tower, does not sit down first and count the cost, whether he has enough to finish it?" (Luke 14:28 NKJV). However, even if we failed to count the costs before we were married, we can still count the costs now.

If you knew ahead of time the sacrifices you would have to make, would you still have chosen your journey of service or of supporting your spouse who serves? Most would say yes. Knowing what to expect can help us prepare for the challenges we may face, but there will still be some surprises along the way. We can't always know the cost, and sometimes the price is higher than we could have anticipated. But we can still have a thriving marriage. In Christ, we are more than conquerors—but we have to turn to him, especially when the costs are high and the future is uncertain.

Even when we try to count the costs, there is only so much we can know about what might happen in the future. In fact, facing the unknown is one of the greatest challenges in life, and it often creates a great deal of anxiety. That's why we train for adversity by immersing ourselves in biblical teaching, prayer, study, and other spiritual disciplines. The wisdom and guidance we need to get off the X comes from God and not from our own knowledge, plans, or desires. We need to draw on that wisdom to address our traumatic experiences, deep wounds, and scars. Left unaddressed, these same wounds will continue to take a toll on our marriages, our parenting, and every other area of our lives.

Yes, your sacrifice has a price, but it also has a reward.

The apostle Paul wrote the following words from prison near the end of his life:

> I want to know Christ and experience the mighty power that raised him from the dead. I want to suffer with him, sharing in his death, so that one way or another I will experience the resurrection from the dead!
>
> I don't mean to say that I have already achieved these things or that I have already reached perfection. But I press on to possess that perfection for which Christ Jesus first possessed me. No, dear brothers and sisters, I have not achieved it, but I focus on this one thing: Forgetting the past and looking forward to what lies ahead, I press on to reach the end of the race and receive the heavenly prize for which God, through Christ Jesus, is calling us. (Philippians 3:10–14 NLT)

Paul sacrificed everything and experienced trauma that included imprisonment, whippings (five times), stoning, beatings (three times), shipwreck (three times), hunger, betrayal, robbery, sleeplessness, lack of clothing, and other dangers (2 Corinthians 11:23–28). Yet he learned to be content in all circumstances. He found divine purpose in his pain and looked toward a heavenly prize waiting for him when he completed his race.

You, too, have a race to run. The Enemy wants trauma to take you out, but it only slowed you down. Until now. It's time to entrust your trauma to God with full confidence that he will not only help you get off the X but will also heal you and reward you for your sacrifice.

Trauma and Stress from God's Perspective

What if you could see your scars and the scars of your spouse as God sees them? As he sees the pain, the tears, the trauma, and all the dark places you're navigating right now? Although we sometimes interpret pain or trauma as a lifelong sentence or as a punishment, God doesn't see it that way. God's view of those who suffer isn't one of condemnation or punishment but of love, mercy, grace, and compassion.

Contrary to what we may have been taught, God isn't sitting in heaven with a hammer waiting to smash us when we sin. Instead, he is waiting patiently for us to come to him for help, for healing, and for hope. He is waiting with loving, open arms for us to come to him with childlike faith, saying, "This is too much for me. Please help me." And when we do, he warmly embraces us. After all, he is the master of taking what is broken, healing it, and using it for good. In God's hands, broken lives become precious vessels used for his glory.

Even if you are suffering from a sense of imminent destruction or paralyzing anxiety, God's peace is available to you. The apostle Paul, who had many reasons to be anxious, described it as a peace that "transcends all understanding" (Philippians 4:7). This peace is the result of surrendering to

God. It is an indicator of his presence in the midst of your pain. This peace is equally available to those who have experienced trauma and to those who love and care for them.

Maybe you are the caregiver of a spouse who served in some capacity and is dealing with lifelong physical injuries or the aftermath of traumatic experiences. Your strength will run dry if you try to serve your spouse only in your own power. Compassion fatigue, a term coined decades ago, was defined by Dr. Charles Figley as a form of secondary trauma.[1] Your compassion has its limits, but the compassion of Christ never runs out. Surrender your burdens to him and ask for his peace.

When we refuse to seek help for PTSD, compassion fatigue, or other challenges often faced by service marriages, we leave the door open for those issues to do ongoing damage in the lives of our spouses and children. Again, if you are the spouse, you are not tasked with healing your warrior. You are tasked with supporting them, guiding them toward professional help, creating a safe place for them, and validating their pain. Seeing your spouse through God's eyes and helping them navigate trauma is one of the most definitive acts of selfless love you can offer a wounded warrior.

A Hope for the Future

At the moment, it may seem like there will be no relief from your pain in the foreseeable future. In fact, the price you have had to pay for your service may seem like a life sentence. But remember, isolation is an Enemy tactic. He wants you to withdraw from loved ones and friends. He wants you to avoid spending time with God and studying his Word. He wants you to isolate yourself, because that's how he keeps you stuck on the X.

The Enemy also wants you to avoid getting help from other resources God has blessed you with, namely doctors, counselors, and other care professionals. These caregivers often play a significant role in God's healing work. Physician Ernest Crocker affirmed the vital connection between faith and modern medicine when he stated:

> Render to scientific medicine the discipline of science and to God and His Word the discipline of faith. . . .
>
> The healing that occurs may be of physical nature but it will always be spiritual and bring hope, peace and cast out fear. It has been said that when God is in the room there is no room for fear. When the doctor has faith he is able to commit his expertise to the Lord in the context of that patient. I believe that he is also able to draw upon God's wisdom and insight.[2]

This is a beautiful reminder of God's grace and provision for our every need. He equips us to serve, and he equips others to help us in our times of need. Our future hope isn't found in isolation; it is found in fellowship and abiding in Christ. God's future for us may not look like what we have in mind, but it will certainly be better than anything we could have imagined on our own. God will use what we have been through for his glory, for our good, and for others to find healing.

Resolve that you will not waver in the face of adversity in your marriage, that you will fight for each other. When you take up your armor and prepare for battle, remember why you are fighting. Your relentless pursuit of a thriving, bulletproof marriage must be tested. Otherwise, what is its worth? With God's help, your marriage will stand the test of time. Whenever you choose to fight for each other, victory is guaranteed.

That doesn't mean the battle will be easy. The Enemy spares no effort when it comes to robbing us of joy, peace, and health in marriage. Marriages and families are his primary targets, and he will use all his assets to take us down. But we have assets of our own. God did not put us here empty-handed. We have the tools we need. We only have to call on him and seek his power and presence to overcome whatever X the Enemy sets in our path.

Together, you can be victorious. But you're going to have to fight for it. Resolve today in your marriage, with each other and with God, that you will fight side by side as one unit until the mission is complete. Look at each other and declare: "I will fight for us, forever."

DISCUSSION

- When have you found yourself on an X in your marriage, recently or in the past? How did you respond?

What, if anything, would you change if you could go back and do things differently?

- What price have you had to pay as a result of trauma? In what ways, if any, does past trauma continue to exact a toll on you and your family?
- From whom are you most likely to isolate when you are in pain? For example, your spouse, family, God and his Word, doctors, counselors, other caregivers. What would you like your spouse to do or not do to create a safe place for you at home?
- What, if anything, stands in the way of you fighting for your marriage?

AFFIRMATION

I will fight for you. I will fight for us. I am grateful for the sacrifices you have made. Our God is a God of hope, and I trust him with our lives and our marriage. I will not try to fix you. I will be with you and support you as you heal. I am with you through all seasons of this life. Now and in all the coming seasons, I promise to serve you, to honor our marriage, and to let God do what only he can do.

ACTION

If you went to the gym for one day and spent twelve hours working out as intensely as possible, you would hope the results would show in the mirror. The reality is that the person who spends twenty minutes a day in the gym four or five days a week, consistently for years, along with healthy eating habits, is the one who sees results. You cannot exercise once and expect to have ripped abs. In the same sense, your marriage cannot be saved by reading a book, putting it down, and going back to the way things were before. Your strength for all seasons of life is rooted in relationship with Christ. If you don't know him as Lord, or as Savior, change that right now.

Conclusion

MARRIAGE ISN'T EASY, BUT IT IS WORTH THE FIGHT. Trauma of any kind creates challenges, and we need the power and presence of God in our lives to overcome those challenges. If you are in the middle of this battle, consider seeking professional help. If you are in the military, a veteran, a first responder, or their spouse, you might consider attending a Mighty Oaks program designed just for you. If you have already overcome your battles with trauma or any other marriage challenge, consider becoming a mentor for other couples. Love for humanity is why God the Father sent his only Son, Jesus, to die for our redemption. It may cost you a little time and effort to support another couple, but I can promise you, that's an investment worth making.

Love will always cost you something you hold dear. But if it draws you closer to the one you love, it is worth whatever the cost may be. If your strength is not based on a relationship with Christ, visit Mighty Oaks Foundation (https://www.mightyoaksprograms.org) and connect with one of our team members who will be happy to talk with you and get you started on this walk. Below is a prayer, which you can use verbatim or as a guideline. Pray together.

> Heavenly Father, we recognize our lives have been tattered with one battle after another, and we cannot do this life without you at the center of it. Today, no matter what has happened in the past, we give our hearts and lives to you. We surrender our marriage to your leadership and ask you to guide us, to give us wisdom, to protect us from the Evil One, and to grant us strength for all seasons as we continue to fight for us, forever. Amen.

What a great honor it would be to hear you have surrendered your life and your marriage to the one who started it all.

Pay It Forward

Kathy and I want the restoration of our marriage to benefit more than us; we also want it to be an illustration of God's love and grace. We have opened our hearts and lives to share our story with you in the hope that it will give you guidance and help lead you closer to the same healing we have experienced. If you are intentional about doing the work and fighting for each other, we believe you will also enjoy God's perfect plan for your marriage.

As you commit to fighting for what matters most, remember that victory doesn't mean you won't have problems. You will always face struggles while on this earth, in life and in marriage. Calibrating your marriage to God's plan isn't a one-and-done kind of operation; you will have to continue to recalibrate your marriage as Satan and the world around you attempt to tear it apart. Stay the course and know the victory has already been won, so long as you are seeking God and fighting for each other.

It's also important to know that victory in Christ and in your marriage is not about you alone; it's about advancing God's kingdom. One of the first things we tell our military warriors at the Mighty Oaks Foundation is, "You think you came here to get well, but that is not the reason you are here. You are here to get well for the purpose of positioning yourself to help the next guy." That is Christ's story, and that is our story. *We must pay it forward.* Paying it forward gives us purpose and accountability and ensures that we continue to grow. The simplest way to pay it forward is to share what God has taught you and what he has done for you. Share where you've been, where you are, and where you are going.

If I were diagnosed with terminal cancer and then found the cure, I couldn't help but share it. My new lease on life would be exhilarating, and the knowledge of this new and unknown cure would be something I'd want everyone to know. I would shout from the rooftops: "Cancer has been defeated, and here's the cure!"

That is how Kathy and I feel about God's restorative

power and covenant plan for marriage. *We can't help but share it.* We now have a new lease on life, and it is exhilarating. That is why we wrote this book—to shout from the rooftops that there is a cure for broken lives and marriages.

Kathy and I are often asked why we continue to be so transparent about our story. We do so because it glorifies God when we share where we came from and where he has brought us. We've come so far from the marriage we once had that sharing our story almost feels like talking about a totally different couple. Plus, we cannot help but think about the divorces and the marriages that are facing their demise now. We want every struggling couple to know about the cure, the truth, the hope, and the restoration God has for them.

We feel compelled, obligated, and led by God to use the very thing that almost destroyed us to minister to others. In the Old Testament story, decades after Joseph's brothers betrayed him, he said, "You intended to harm me, but God intended it for good" (Genesis 50:20). This same story played out in our lives. The destruction the Enemy planned for us was redirected by God to be used for his good. We have been blessed to see others inspired and then find hope and restoration in Christ through the story God has written in our marriage. If we tap into the cure through our relationship with Jesus Christ, Satan can no longer destroy life, love, and the joy God intended for marriage.

Our challenge for you is to continue to pay it forward. We did not keep this cure a secret when we received it. We have and will continue to share it, and we hope you will too. Pass this book on to another couple and help them work through its principles. One of the greatest gifts in the Christian walk is mentorship, through which we share God's truth and encourage others to do the same. That is the model of discipleship—to lead others, to continue to mentor, and to pass on the truth and wisdom. Don't let this gift end with you!

To pay it forward, you don't have to have your life and marriage all figured out or have all the answers. You simply have to use your own testimony to point others to the one who does have all the answers. Always remember that your testimony is not about what you are doing, but what Christ did at the cross for you and how he is continuing to love and heal you today.

Acknowledgments

CHAD ROBICHAUX: I would like to dedicate this book to my wife, Kathy, who fought for me when I couldn't even fight for myself, and to my amazing children, Hunter, Haili, and Hayden, who have always given me the will to stay in the fight. Special thanks to Steve and Babbette Toth for the love and mentorship that led me from darkness to light, and to my team at Mighty Oaks Foundation who has locked arms with me to pay it forward to the world and to challenge others to do the same.

ADAM DAVIS: I would like to thank Dianne Krylo and the late Mr. Kevin Krylo for their gracious investment in my life and mission to reach others for Christ. A special thanks to Lt. Col. Dave Grossman for the many hours of conversation and for challenging me to improve my sleep.

APPENDIX A

WISDOM AND HEALTHY HABITS FOR MARRIAGE

A FEW YEARS BACK, MY COAUTHOR ADAM DAVIS met two chaplains from the Billy Graham Evangelistic Association, Dianne and Kevin Krylo. While Adam and the Krylos were ministering to first responders in Texas, Kevin gave Adam a piece of paper detailing two simple tools he and Dianne used to counsel and minister to couples over the years. They were questions for drawing closer to each other and ten habits of happy couples. Although Kevin died in 2020 after a battle with cancer, we are blessed to have Dianne's permission to share these powerful tools with you. Kevin and Dianne, this is for your legacy—a legacy of kingdom work that lives on.

Questions for Drawing Closer to Each Other

Three questions about last week

- What did I do to make you feel loved this week?
- How did I do at showing my appreciation for you?
- Did you see any answered prayers this past week?

Three questions for the weekend

- What burden are you carrying that we can manage together?
- What will we do this weekend to focus on our marriage?
- How would you best feel pursued by me?

Three questions about next week

- What does the coming week look like for you?
- What's the best thing I can do to let you know that you are my priority and my joy?
- How can I pray for you in the coming week?

Bonus

- How do you see God at work in my/our life?

Ten Habits of Happy Couples

1. Pray together every day; meaningful, uninterrupted prayer.
2. Say "I love you" and "Have a good day" every morning.
3. Cultivate common interests.
4. Walk hand in hand or side by side.
5. Be proud to be seen with your spouse.
6. Make trust and forgiveness your default mode.
7. Focus more on what your partner does right than what your partner does wrong.
8. Do a "weather check" during the day; call to see how your spouse is doing.
9. Hug each other for two minutes as soon as you see each other after work. Say good night every night, regardless of how you feel.
10. Go to bed at the same time whenever possible.

Nine Tips for Building a Stronger Marriage

1. Attend church together.
2. Pray together daily.
3. Spend twenty minutes a day in face-to-face dialogue.
4. Read the Bible together at least once a week.
5. Let your children know that both of you need time alone together.
6. Commit to making important decisions together.
7. When running errands together, turn off the radio in the car (or other electronic devices if walking) and talk to each other.
8. When traveling together, don't take work on the plane or the road. Spend time talking instead.

9. Continue dating:
   - Set aside regular times to continue developing your romance. Having an evening or an afternoon out together twice a month is a good start.
   - Arrange for a quiet evening at home together once a month.
   - Hire a babysitter to watch the kids for a couple of hours even though you are home. This works wonders!
   - Work out a deal with another couple to trade off watching each other's kids overnight so you can both have an evening alone.

NOTES

CHAPTER 1: NEVER QUIT ON US

1. Nikki Wentling, "VA Reveals Its Veteran Suicide Statistic Included Active-Duty Troops," *Stars and Stripes*, June 21, 2018, https://www.stripes.com/news/us/va-reveals-its -veteran-suicide-statistic-included-active-duty-troops -1.533992.
2. Johns Hopkins Medicine, "Children Who Lose a Parent to Suicide More Likely to Die the Same Way," news release, April 21, 2010, www.hopkinsmedicine.org/news/media /releases/children_who_lose_a_parent_to_suicide_more _likely_to_die_the_same_way.
3. Blaise Pascal, "Morality and Doctrine," in *Thoughts, Letters, and Minor Works*, ed. Charles W. Eliot, trans. W. F. Trotter, vol. 48 (New York: P. F. Collier & Son, 1910), 138–39.

CHAPTER 2: THE SOURCE OF LOVE

1. "Marine Corps Values," Life as a Marine, Marines (website), accessed April 6, 2021, https://www.marines.com /life-as-a-marine/standards/values.html.

CHAPTER 3: FULLY COMMITTED

1. Drs. Les and Leslie Parrott, *The Complete Guide to Marriage Mentoring: Connecting Couples to Build Better Marriages* (Grand Rapids, MI: Zondervan, 2005), 176.

2. Andy Stanley, "Congratulations!," Twitter, August 6, 2018, 11:56 a.m., https://twitter.com/AndyStanley /status/1026497156453154816.

CHAPTER 4: PREPARE FOR BATTLE

1. Dennis and Barbara Rainey, *Starting Your Marriage Right: What You Need to Know and Do in the Early Years to Make It Last a Lifetime* (Nashville: Nelson Books, 2000), 21.

2. Lou Holtz, *Three Rules for Living a Good Life: A Game Plan for After Graduation* (Notre Dame, IN: Ave Maria Press, 2019), xv.

CHAPTER 5: OVERCOMING EVIL

1. Melissa Merrick et al., "Prevalence of Adverse Childhood Experiences from the 2011–2014 Behavioral Risk Factor Surveillance System in 23 States," *JAMA Pediatrics* 172, no. 11 (November 2018): 1038–44, https://doi.org/10.1001 /jamapediatrics.2018.2537.

2. "Post-Traumatic Stress Disorder (PTSD)," Mayo Clinic, July 6, 2018, https://www.mayoclinic.org/diseases -conditions/post-traumatic-stress-disorder/symptoms -causes/syc-20355967.

3. Centers for Disease Control and Prevention, "Suicide Rising Across the US," *VitalSigns*, June 7, 2018, www.cdc.gov /vitalsigns/suicide/index.html.

4. Andrew Christensen, Brian D. Doss, and Neil S. Jacobson, *Reconcilable Differences*, 2nd ed. (New York: The Guilford Press, 2014), 135.

5. Amy Bushatz, "PTSD and Marriage: 5 Things Spouses Need to Know," Military.com, accessed May 8, 2021, www .military.com/spouse/relationships/military-marriage/ptsd -and-marriage-4-things-spouses-need-to-know.html.
6. Frank D. Fincham, Julie Hall, and Steven R. H. Beach, "Forgiveness in Marriage: Current Status and Future Directions," *Family Relations* 55, no. 4 (June 2006): 415–27, https://doi.org/10.1111/j.1741-3729.2005.callf.x-i1.
7. Lewis B. Smedes, "Forgiveness—The Power to Change the Past," *Christianity Today*, January 7, 1983, https://www .christianitytoday.com/ct/2002/decemberweb-only/12 -16-55.0.html.
8. Terry Gaspard, "How Forgiveness Can Transform Your Marriage," Gottman Institute, December 29, 2016, www .gottman.com/blog/forgiveness-can-transform-marriage/.

CHAPTER 6: LIFE PIVOT

1. Winston S. Churchill, *Churchill by Himself*, ed. Richard M. Langworth (2008; repr., New York: Public Affairs, 2011), 13; and "Churchill Quotes Without Credit," Churchill Project, February 5, 2016, https://winstonchurchill .hillsdale.edu/churchill-quotes-without-credit/.
2. Larissa Rainey, "The Search for Purpose in Life: An Exploration of Purpose, the Search Process, and Purpose Anxiety" (master's thesis, University of Pennsylvania, 2014), http://repository.upenn.edu/mapp_capstone/60.
3. Tony Evans, "Looking for Your Purpose?" Urban Alternative, accessed May 8, 2021, https://go.tonyevans.org /blog/looking-for-your-purpose.
4. "I'm Getting Older. How Do I Find My Purpose?" Billy Graham Evangelistic Association, August 19, 2019, https://billygraham .org/answer/im-getting-older-how-do-i-find-my-purpose/.

5. Donald Miller, "Part 1: Don Miller on Directing Your New Story (Enneagram 3) [S02–014]," interview by Ian Cron, November 1, 2018, *Typology* podcast, https://www.typologypodcast.com/podcast/2018/28/06/episode2-014/donmiller.

CHAPTER 7: FUEL FOR THE FIGHT

1. *Merriam-Webster*, s.v. "Bridegroom," accessed May 9, 2021, https://www.merriam-webster.com/dictionary/bridegroom.
2. Michael J. Wilkins, *The NIV Application Commentary: Matthew*, ed. Terry Muck (Grand Rapids, MI: Zondervan, 2004), 642–43.
3. Lt. Col. Dave Grossman, in conversations with author Adam Davis.
4. Brian C. Tefft, "Acute Sleep Deprivation and Culpable Motor Vehicle Crash Involvement," *Sleep* 41, no. 10 (October 2018), https://doi.org/10.1093/sleep/zsy144.
5. Rebecca A. Bernert and Thomas E. Joiner, "Sleep Disturbances and Suicide Risk: A Review of the Literature," *Neuropsychiatric Disease and Treatment* 3, no. 6 (January 2008), https://doi.org/10.2147/NDT.S1248.
6. Eugene M. Bartlett, "Victory in Jesus" (1939; repr., Powell, MO: Albert E. Brumley & Sons, Inc., 1967).

CHAPTER 8: ACCESSING THE POWER

1. R. Kent Hughes, *Disciplines of a Godly Man*, rev. ed. (Wheaton, IL: Crossway, 2019), 77.
2. Christopher Marlowe, *Doctor Faustus* (London: Oxberry, 1818), 14.
3. Max Lucado, *Experiencing the Heart of Jesus* (Nashville: Thomas Nelson, 2003), 10.
4. Mark Batterson, *Whisper: How to Hear the Voice of God* (Colorado Springs, CO: Multnomah, 2017), 174.

5. Dallas Willard, "Willard Words," Dallas Willard (website), accessed May 9, 2021, http://old.dwillard.org/resources /WillardWords.asp.

CHAPTER 9: JESUS FIRST . . . ALWAYS

1. Stu Weber, *Tender Warrior: Every Man's Purpose, Every Woman's Dream, Every Child's Hope*, rev. ed. (Colorado Springs, CO: Multnomah, 2006), 214.
2. "Our Story," I Am Second, accessed May 9, 2021, https://www.iamsecond.com/our-story/.

CHAPTER 10: STRENGTH FOR ALL SEASONS

1. Charles R. Figley, "Compassion Fatigue as Secondary Traumatic Stress Disorder: An Overview," in *Compassion Fatigue: Coping with Secondary Traumatic Stress Disorder in Those Who Treat the Traumatized*, ed. Charles R. Figley (New York: Routledge, 1995), 1–20.
2. Sami K. Martin, "Dr. Ernest Crocker on Faith and Healing: 'Modern Medicine Is a Gift from God,'" *Christian Post*, July 9, 2013, http://www.christianpost.com/news/dr-ernest -crocker-on-faith-and-healing-modern-medicine-is-a-gift -from-god-99680/.

About the Authors

Chad M. Robichaux, BCPC, MBA

Chad is a former Force Recon Marine and DoD contractor with eight deployments to Afghanistan as part of a Joint Special Operations Command (JSOC) task force. After overcoming his personal battles with PTSD and nearly becoming a veteran suicide statistic, Chad founded the Mighty Oaks Foundation, a leading nonprofit serving the active duty and military veteran communities with highly successful faith-based combat trauma and resiliency programs. Having spoken to over 250,000 active-duty troops and led life-saving programs for over 4,500 active-duty and military veterans at four Mighty Oaks Ranches around the nation, Chad has become a go-to resource and is considered an expert on faith-based solutions to PTSD. He has advised the former presidential administration, Congress, the VA, and the DoD, and was appointed to serve as the chairman of a White House veterans coalition.

Chad is a bestselling author and has written six books related to veteran care, donating over 150,000 copies to the troops during his resiliency speaking tours. He is regularly featured on national media and has been a contributor to Fox News, Newsmax, and Blaze Media. Chad's story was notably shared in a short film by I Am Second and the documentary *Never Fight Alone*. Currently, a motion picture is being produced based on Chad and Kathy's story.

In addition to Chad's military service, he is a former federal agent and law enforcement officer who was awarded the Medal of Valor for bravery. Chad has been married to his wife, Kathy, for twenty-six years, and they have a daughter and two sons. Hunter and Hayden are both third-generation marines in the Robichaux family and share Chad's passion as lifelong martial artists. Chad is also a fourth-degree Brazilian jiu-jitsu black belt under Carlson Gracie Jr. and a former professional mixed martial arts champion, having competed at the highest levels of the sport. Chad's books include *An Unfair Advantage*, *Path to Resiliency*, *The Truth About PTSD*, and the military devotional *Behind the Lines*.

Adam Davis

Adam is a former law enforcement officer and an FBI-trained hostage negotiator. Since leaving his career in law enforcement in 2015, he has devoted his life to serving others by developing personal growth resources and inspiring others to make positive changes through his writing and speaking. He has been described as an unrelenting force of inspiration and believes we all have a unique purpose and that we must be good stewards of the time we are given in this life.

Adam has an uncanny ability to speak "grunt" and to the heart of warriors. He has shared his story of overcoming trauma—including childhood sexual abuse, experiences in law enforcement, battles with suicidal thoughts, and substance abuse—with audiences at major universities, law enforcement agencies, military bases, and conferences. His work has attracted the attention of many influencers, and he is best known for delivering faith, hope, and love to those who serve.

Adam's writing has been featured in *Entrepreneur* magazine, Fox News, HuffPost, Police1, and Law Enforcement Today. As a speaker, he has presented for the University of Alabama, Auburn University's Government and Economic Development Institute, TEDx, Troy University, law enforcement agencies, military bases, and at many seminars with Lt. Col. Dave Grossman, Taya Kyle, and other American patriots. His media appearances include Newsmax, *Rick and Bubba Show*, Blaze Radio Network, *FamilyLife Today*, *700 Club*, *Glenn Beck Program*, *Team Never Quit* podcast, and many others.

Adam is the spokesperson for REBOOT First Responders, a course with the nonprofit organization REBOOT Recovery, which focuses on providing faith-based trauma healing for first responders and service members.

Adam's books include *Behind the Badge: 365 Daily Devotions for Law Enforcement, Bulletproof Marriage: A 90-Day Devotional* (with Lt. Col. Dave Grossman), and *On Spiritual Combat: 30 Missions for Victorious Warfare* (with Lt. Col. Dave Grossman).

Adam and his wife, Amber, reside in Alabama with their three children.c dr

Mighty Oaks Foundation

Chad Robichaux founded the Mighty Oaks Foundation, a leading nonprofit, serving the active-duty and military veteran communities with highly successful faith-based combat trauma and resiliency programs. Having spoken to over 250,000 active-duty troops and led life-saving programs for over 4,000 active military and veterans at four Mighty Oaks Ranches around the nation, Chad has become a go-to resource and is considered a subject matter expert on faith-based solutions to PTSd. He has advised the former presidential administration, Congress, the VA, the DoD, and was appointed to serve as the chairman of a White House veterans coalition.

About Our Programs

The Mighty Oaks Warrior journey begins with intensive peer-based programs that utilize instructional sessions, camaraderie, and team-building activities that are designed to challenge our Warriors to overcome their past experiences

and move forward into a life of purpose. Our programs take place all across America on military bases, at our outposts, and on rural ranch lodges. Each facility allows the Warriors to appreciate the peace of nature and have an "unplugged" experience while they focus on the challenges they face in completing the program.

MIGHTY OAKS
★ FOUNDATION ★

Learn More & Get Involved Today
MightyOaksPrograms.org

Legacy Program for Men

Our five-day intensive peer-to-peer program serves as the catalyst to help Warriors discover the answers to the big questions in life. Challenges related to the struggles of daily military life, combat deployments, and the symptoms of post-traumatic stress (PTS) surface during these five days. This program teaches how to identify and fight through the challenges that might have been limiting personal success.

Legacy Program for Women

This program identifies and confronts the daily struggles of dealing with current or post military life, as well as PTS that stems from life, job, or military experiences. This four-day program, leads spouses, active-duty military service members, veterans, and first-responders through a time of learning, exploration, and growth with the aim to cultivate spiritual strength of character in a safe, open, and nurturing environment.

Mighty Oaks provides peer-to-peer resiliency and recovery programs that serve as the catalyst to assist our nation's Warriors dealing with challenges related to the struggles of daily military life, combat deployments, and the symptoms of post-traumatic stress (PTS), offered at **no-cost** to our nation's Warriors, including travel to beautiful ranches across the United States.

Apply Today

MightyOaksPrograms.org

Save Our Allies is a veteran and military support coalition focused on delivering full and timely benefits to the U.S. military community in need, and ensuring Afghan personnel and their families who supported our U.S. forces are properly protected from violence and persecution by evacuation to safe countries, including the United States.

Save Our Allies is dedicated to saving our Afghan allies who served side-by-side with U.S. Armed Forces and work to ensure our veterans are getting the care they need after bravely serving our nation.

Learn More & Support Our Mission

SaveOurAllies.org